AL GAR VE

Travel with Marco Polo
Insider Tips

INSIDER TIP
Your shortcut
to a great
experience

MARCO POLO
TOP HIGHLIGHTS

ALBUFEIRA ⭐
The best beaches in the area. Lots of great cafés, bars and restaurants. And there's even a marina.

➤ p. 76, The Barlavento

CULATRA ⭐
Take the ferry to the traffic-free islands of Culatra and Armona. Far from the bustle of the coast, it is a whole different world out there.

➤ p. 52, The Sotavento

LAGOS ⭐
This is where Henry the Navigator wrote his buccaneering adventure stories. Today its charm comes from the port and the atmospheric old city.

➤ p. 68, The Barlavento

TAVIRA ⭐
A stunning town of many churches on the Rio Gilão.
📷 *Tip: At the Praia do Barril on the Ilha de Tavira, the huge graveyard of anchors in the sand makes an epic subject for photos.*

➤ p. 53, The Sotavento

FARO'S VILA-ADENTRO (OLD TOWN) ⭐
In the middle of the buzzing modern city, Faro's old town – with its cathedral, monastery and web of tiny lanes – feels a bit like a museum.

➤ p. 42, The Sotavento

IGREJA DE SÃO LOURENÇO ⭐
The Baroque church in Almancil has some of the best examples of *azulejo* tiles in the region. The rich, golden decoration provides a clear sense of Portugal's colonial wealth.

➤ p. 48, The Sotavento

LOULÉ

The neo-Moorish covered market is the jewel of this pretty inland town. There is also an impressive fortress up on the hill.

📷 *Tip: Come here in the mornings when the fish traders are still spread out all over the market and the surrounding areas. It's the best way to make sure you get a slice of real life in your photos!*

➤ p. 120, The Hinterland

SERRA DE MONCHIQUE ⑧

The so-called Garden of the Algarve is the beautiful countryside around the small mountain village of Monchique.

📷 *Tip: Climb on to the rocks at the summit of Fóia for the best views down towards the coast.*

➤ p. 115, The Hinterland

ARRIFANA ⑨

The Costa Vicentina's stunning steep cliffs are enough to take anyone's breath away.

📷 *Tip: For great surfing pictures, head to Arrifana beach, where the waves are so high you can see them from the car park.*

➤ p. 106, The West Coast

CABO DE SÃO VICENTE ⑩

Mainland Europe's most south-westerly point, this cape gets battered by wind and waves (photo).

📷 *Tip: As the sun begins its daily descent and the lighthouse is bathed in golden evening light, there is no better place to be.*

➤ p. 101, The West Coast

CONTENTS

THE WEST COAST   THE HINTERLAND   THE SOTAVENTO   THE BARLAVENTO

CONTENTS

⏱	Plan your visit	🍴	Eating/drinking	☂	Rainy day activities
€ – €€€	Price categories	🛍	Shopping	🐷	Budget activities
(*)	Premium-rate phone number	⛾	Going out	👥	Family activities
		🏖	Top beaches	⚑	Classic experiences

(*A2*) Refers to the removable pull-out map
(0) Located off the map

BEST OF ALGARVE

A natural masterpiece: the Benagil sea cave near Carvoeiro

BEST ☂
WHEN IT RAINS

ACTIVITIES TO BRIGHTEN YOUR DAY

SHELTER IN THE CONVENT
The *Convento Nossa Senhora da Assunção* in the old part of Faro now houses the city's museum. Its wonderful cloisters and the surrounding rooms provide the perfect shelter from the rain.
➤ p. 43, The Sotavento

HIT THE SHOPS
On rainy days, the Algarve's shopping centres draw in people like powerful magnets. Whether it's *Forum Algarve* in Faro, *Algarve Shopping* in Guia or the *Aqua Portimão*, all these centres have plenty to fill a damp day, from shops to restaurants, cinemas and more.
➤ p. 46, The Sotavento, p. 82 and p. 88, The Barlovento

MAKE YOURSELF AT HOME IN A BEACH BAR
Wooden snack bars can be found on just about every beach. You can sit in them for hours, have a few drinks, read, or simply daydream. If the weather changes and the sea is rough, *Praia da Galé's* beach restaurants are particularly cosy places to seek shelter.
➤ p. 80, The Barlavento

JUST DIVE IN
The rain won't bother you if you're getting wet anyway. The *Subnauta* team in Portimão will take you to the most beautiful diving spots and shipwrecks on the Algarve coast. Beginners are also welcome.
➤ p. 89, The Barlavento

MORE THAN A LOCAL MUSEUM
There are lots of things to see and do in the *Museu do Traje* in São Brás de Alportel: the museum's display of traditional dress and costumes, a cork exhibition in an adjacent building and, last but not least, the museum's bar.
➤ p. 125, The Hinterland

BEST 🐷
ON A BUDGET

FOR SMALLER WALLETS

HILLTOP CASTLE
Perched on a hill, the *Castelo* dominates Tavira and its landscape. There is no admission fee to visit the castle walls, so free your inner child for a few hours and clamber around while enjoying the stunning views.
➤ p. 55, The Sotavento

BUY FROM THE GROWERS
Do your bit by supporting local people. Some locals sell produce they have picked from their fruit trees or vegetable patches at rock-bottom prices in front of their houses.
➤ p. 79, The Barlavento

SUNDAY AT THE MUSEUM
Housed in a former sardine factory, the municipal *Museu de Portimão* offers a fascinating insight into working life over the last century, and you can visit for free on Sunday afternoons. In August, it is open until 11pm.
➤ p. 85, The Barlavento

A BEACON AT THE WORLD'S END
On Wednesday afternoons, the keeper of the *Cabo de São Vicente* lighthouse will guide you through his place of work for free; simply wait until he opens the door and lets in the next group of people (photo).
➤ p. 101, The West Coast

WATER STRAIGHT FROM THE SOURCE
The *Serra de Monchique* is home to lots of natural springs. Do what the locals do and fill your bottles and flasks whenever you can.
➤ p. 116 and p 120, The Hinterland

CHAPEL TEEMING WITH TILES
The *Ermida Nossa Senhora da Conceição* in the historic centre of Loulé is adorned with the most spectacular *azulejos*. You can enjoy this delightful chapel for free.
➤ p. 121, The Hinterland

BEST
WITH CHILDREN

FUN FOR YOUNG & OLD

STUDYING STARFISH

The *Centro Ciência Viva do Algarve* is the kind of interactive museum that will get the whole family enthused. You will come out with an in-depth understanding of how the *lagunas* on the Ria Formosa were formed … and of what lives in them, from sea cucumbers to hermit crabs and starfish.

➤ p. 44, The Sotavento

CANOPY CLIMBING

Carabiner secure? Belt tight? Then tally-ho and up to the treetops you (or your kids) go! The high-rope courses at the *Parque Aventura* in Albufeira have something for kids of all ages – from toddler trails up to courses for "adventurers" and "the fearless".

➤ p. 60, The Sotavento

A DAY AT THE ZOO

Lemurs, with their long tails and huge eyes, can put a smile on the face of even the grumpiest toddler. Alongside the lemurs, the *Zoo de Lagos* has an impressive collection of exotic primates and birds, as well as native sheep and goats and a petting zoo.

➤ p. 74, The Barlavento

GET WET & GO WILD

The clue is in the name at *Slide & Splash*, a waterpark that shows you just how many ways there are to enter the water (some are seriously fast). Make sure your swimsuit doesn't slip down too easily (you will thank us!) and then jump in.

➤ p. 89, The Barlavento

BRIBING DONKEYS

You won't get far on a *donkey trek* if you don't have any carrots to bribe your trusty – but often pretty stubborn – steed. So long as you can keep them going, a donkey trek is a treat for all the family and the Costa Vicentina has plenty of great routes to explore.

➤ p. 104, The West Coast

SMALL WORKS OF ART

Azulejos, painted ceramic tiles, are Portugal's most beautiful contribution to the art world. Their name and origin date back to the Moors: *az-zulayi* means "small stone". They decorate courtyards, hospitals and churches, such as the *Igreja de São Lourenço* in Almancil.
➤ p. 48, The Sotavento

BLUE BEACHES

Blue flags fluttering in the wind guarantee a clean stretch of Algarve coastline, and the pristine white beaches are great adverts for the system. The showcase beach has to be the *Praia da Falésia* near Albufeira.
➤ p. 79, The Barlavento

BEACH PARTY

Summertime is party time in the coastal towns along the Algarve, and things get especially wild on the *Praia da Rocha* in Portimão.
➤ p. 89, The Barlavento

POSTCARD PERFECT

Bold, bright boats for fishermen (photo). Even the large yachts that you see in every harbour are a display of colour. The most postcard-worthy harbour is in *Sagres*.
➤ p. 98, The West Coast

SURFERS' HAVEN

Because huge waves generate huge fun, surfers are drawn to the Atlantic coast all year round – conditions here are also good for wind – and kitesurfers. Top hot spot: *Praia da Bordeira*.
➤ p. 107, The West Coast

MOUNTAIN FIREWATER

Strawberries on bushes? The fruit of the strawberry tree looks convincingly like a strawberry, but these berries are not to be eaten. Instead they are fermented to produce *medronho*. Try it: the strong spirit has a superb taste.
➤ p. 119, The Hinterland

GET TO KNOW ALGARVE

Spring in the Algarve means storks nesting on the rooftops and on the city gate in Faro.

DISCOVER ALGARVE

Jacaranda trees in bloom below Silves cathedral and castle

Many, many hours of sunshine, clean seawater, heavenly beaches, sheltered coves, rocky cliffs and sand dunes galore. If you search for "holiday" online, you might well find a picture taken in the Algarve. And if relaxing on a beach for two weeks is not for you, there is much more to this region than just its glorious sun and sand.

SUMMERS OF SUNSHINE

In summer the whole of the Algarve buzzes with activity. The warm evenings are accompanied by music emanating from the many bars, and in the villages in the hinterland there is always some kind of festival going on. If you like an action-packed holiday, you'll find plenty to do on the coast, from surfing to kayaking. It may seem too hot for hiking, but in the mountains and on the west coast you will

1100 BCE
Phoenician settlers build the first ports on the coast

218 BCE–CE 400
The Iberian Peninsula is under Roman rule

711–1249
The period of Moorish rule

1419
Under Prince Henry the Navigator the "Era of Discovery" begins

1580–1640
Portugal becomes a vassal state held by the Spanish

1755
Severe earthquake destroys many towns and cities

1910

often find a refreshing breeze. And the amusement parks are open every day during the summer, so you can channel your inner child as you ride the waterslides. From May to October you will rarely find anything closed, as the bars and restaurants all make hay while the sun very literally shines. Beware: it can get very busy here, as the Portuguese also love their south coast and, during August, half the country descends on the Algarve for a few days' holiday …

THE CALM MIDWINTER

If you travel outside the school holidays or decide not to spend all your time swimming and sunbathing, you will experience a whole other side to the Algarve. Things quickly quieten down during the autumn, while in winter some people find it a little too quiet – especially once many of the bars and restaurants have gone into hibernation. This time of year is perfect for golfers, as well as hikers, cyclists and people looking for peace and quiet. In winter on the Algarve, temperatures can hover at a wonderful 20°C for weeks on end.

THE COLOURS OF SPRING

But it has to rain sometimes, or there wouldn't be so many stunning fields of flowers in spring and summer. Even during the colder half of the year you can find plenty of flora – from pure white almond blossom to glowing yellow acacia groves and the purple-spotted rock rose; and the usually barren coastal macchia suddenly bursts forth in a vibrant green – not to mention the hills of the hinterland, which can seem almost desert-like in summer. The winter also offers

End of the monarchy. Proclamation of the Republic

1932–74 From the Salazar dictatorship to the "Carnation Revolution"

1986 Portugal joins the European Community

2012–14 Economic crisis: Portugal receives EU bail-out package

2017 Faro airport reopens after years of reconstruction work; it now processes eight million passengers a year

2018 The first exploratory oil-drilling operations begin on the west coast

INSIDER TIP
Frolicking flamingos

superb birdwatching, as so many migratory birds spend the winter here. During the spring the birds flutter between the rooftops, and from March onwards it is difficult to find an electricity pylon that doesn't have a stork's nest on top of it.

SURPRISING DIVERSITY

Whatever time of year you visit the Algarve, it's worth exploring all the different regions in the province and their extraordinary diversity. The best way to do this is to rent a car. Often just a few kilometres separate the buzzing coastal towns from secluded mountain villages; the tranquil coves on the rocky coast are less than an hour away from the rough and untamed west coast; and, from the beautiful towns of the eastern Algarve, it's just a short boat trip across the lagoons of the Ria Formosa to the almost endless sandy beaches of the barrier islands.

ALL WELL IN PARADISE?

The isolated mountain villages may seem picturesque but rural exodus is a serious problem – especially when it's only the older people who stay behind. The fishing industry is no longer able to support the population here and Portugal's 2010–2014 economic crisis hit the Algarve hard. Even though tourism may be booming once again, it is fundamentally a seasonal industry. A lot of mistakes have been made in the tourism business too, as evidenced by numerous unfinished buildings and concrete monstrosities along parts of the coasts. It remains to be seen whether oil drilling off the coast will become the latest in a series of poor economic bets for the region. Algarvios display an irrepressible Mediterranean nonchalance – come what may, they simply make the best out of the situation.

DEEP SOUTH OR FAR WEST?

But what exactly is the homeland of the Algarvios? It's the southernmost tip of Portugal, stretching like an elongated rectangle from the Spanish border to the Atlantic coast in the west. The 150-km-long southern coastline is naturally divided into two halves: in the west, the dramatic, rocky coast of the Barlavento; and in the east, the Sotavento, characterised by enormous beaches with dunes and lagoons. To the north of this lies a sometimes fertile, sometimes barren landscape of hills and mountains that extends around 50km to the border with the neighbouring province of Alentejo. The official name for the Algarve is the rather uninspiring *Distrito de Faro* – it is just one of 17 administrative districts in Portugal, and is simply named after its regional capital. However, the Moors who ruled over the region from the eighth until the 13th century came up with a more beautiful-sounding name: *Al-Gharb*, meaning "the West", as this was the westernmost part of their Caliphate on the Iberian Peninsula. They were very reluctant to submit to the Christian Reconquista; you may well find yourself as reluctant to leave as they were all those centuries ago.

AT A GLANCE

451,006
population

Leeds 474,632

200km
Coastline

Pembrokeshire coastline: 299km

4,997km²
Total area

Kent: 3,736km²

HIGHEST MOUNTAIN:
FÓIA

902M

WARMEST & MOST POPULAR MONTH

AUGUST 28°C

HOURS OF SUN PER YEAR

3,000

LONDON: 1,410

AREA WITH THE MOST EXPENSIVE HOTELS

Quinta do Lago (approx. 500 euros for a double room in August in the Hotel Conrad Algarve)

GOLF

36 golf courses
Scotland: 550

BRITS' PARTY AREA
"The Strip" (Av. Dr Francisco Sá Carneiro, Albufeira)

FRUIT NEEDED TO MAKE 1 LITRE OF *MEDRONHO*: 8KG

UNDERSTAND ALGARVE

THE MOUNTAINS ARE CALLING

For many years, it was the seaside that beckoned, as native Algarvios flooded from the hinterland into the rapidly expanding coastal towns in pursuit of promising job opportunities in the booming tourism industry. Life on the coast seemed more appealing than working in the region's back-breaking traditional agricultural industry; only the elderly were left behind in their villages, and some areas are now virtually deserted. Attempts, such as the Via Algarviana long-distance hiking trail, have been made to attract tourists to these remote regions. However, they have – as yet – only achieved modest success in bringing life back to the villages. And yet these are remarkable places, situated within a stunning hilly landscape – sometimes barren, sometimes covered in cork oak forests, and criss-crossed with fantastic hiking trails. Make sure you head up into the Serra do Caldeirão or the Serra de Monchique for a walk, and afterwards pop into one of the remaining traditional village taverns for a glass of *medronho* with the locals. You won't regret it.

INSIDER TIP
Get in the spirit!

CORK CRAZE

Every bottle of Portuguese wine is sealed with real cork, and the craze for this natural, waterproof product does not stop there. Walk into a souvenir shop and you will encounter cork products of every imaginable kind, from postcards to finely carved sculptures. To discover why there is so much interest in this ancient material, take a trip into the Serra de Monchique, where beautiful ancient trees shed one layer of cork cells every nine years. The cork farmers keep track of when each tree is due a harvest by writing the year of the last harvest on the trunk. This is no way to make a quick buck … nonetheless the Portuguese have turned cork into one of their most important exports and are the world's biggest producer. If you are interested in learning how to turn bark into bottle stoppers, the processing plant in São Brás de Alportel offers guided tours.

GLEAMING WALLS

Tilers in Portugal during the 18th and 19th centuries must have been exhausted – there is hardly a church in the whole country that isn't decorated with *azulejos* … Particularly splendid examples from this period include the Igreja de São Lourenço, on the edge of Almancil, and the Igreja de Santo António, in Lagos. However, the tradition is much older, and was originally introduced by the Moors, who gave these tiles their name: *al-zulij*, or "small stone". The tiles are frequently painted in blue and white (although more colourful examples can also be found) and are more than just attractive decorative objects – they also serve as a heat- and weather-resistant wall lining.

Cork oak bark waits to be turned into bottle stoppers in São Bras

SMALL FRY

You can find fresh fish on the menu in every restaurant, which makes sense – we are on the coast here, after all. But is all this fish really caught locally? The bream and sea bass generally come from fish farms, the *bacalhau* (dried cod) is imported from Norway, and the only relics of the golden age of tuna fishing are the former factories (now converted into tourist attractions), like those in Quatro Águas or on the Praia do Barril in Tavira. The formerly wide-spread fish-canning industry has also been reduced to just two canneries. However, if you pay a visit to the fishing ports of Olhão, Portimão, Quarteira, Alvor or Sagres, you will see that there are still fresh fish to be caught – as well as men working hard to catch them. This is particularly the case in summer,

which is sardine season. Both the ports and the indoor fish markets paint a vivid picture of this industry, which was the region's most important right up until the 20th century. Incidentally, the bright colours of the fishing boats were primarily for safety – to make them more visible in the fog – rather than aesthetics.

LIVING LAGOON

You probably caught an initial glimpse of the enormous Ria Formosa – with its mud flats, channels, sandbanks, rows of dunes and salt marshes – from your plane on the way into Faro airport, as the flight path cuts directly across this 170-km² nature park. The many birds that inhabit this protected area have grown accustomed to their huge metal counterparts flying overhead and seem unfazed by them. However, you may find yourself overwhelmed by this remarkable natural feature. The Ria Formosa is a lagoon landscape measuring around 60km in length, making it one of the biggest and most beautiful in Europe. The area is separated from the sea by enormous and animals (especially birds). The nature park centre *Quinta de Marim* in Olhão also offers plenty of information about the origins of the *ria* and the many living creatures that can be found there, with a well-designed nature trail leading across the premises.

Is it a church tower? Is it a minaret? No, it's a typical Algarvian chimney!

sandbanks, and at high tide it transforms into an intricate network of rivulets, channels and marshes. The sandbanks themselves are lined with seemingly endless idyllic beaches, a few of which are inhabited – generally by cockle-pickers and fishermen. Some are accessible via a causeway, while others can only be reached by boat. It is well worth taking a guided boat tour through the *ria*, as you will see a whole host of unusual plants

ORNATE CHIMNEYS

It is hardly surprising that these distinctive chimneys have become an emblem of sorts for the Algarve. Some are round, others oblong. It doesn't matter whether the house is old or new – chimneys give houses in the Algarve character. Historians suspect they were originally camouflaged minarets, from the time when the region was claimed back from the Moors and Christianity was enforced with a vengeance.

MANUEL THE MAGNIFICENT

King Manuel I was known as "the Fortunate", as during his reign Portugal experienced the high point of its global fame and wealth thanks to the voyages of exploration led by Vasco da Gama and other seafarers. Portugal became a central figure in the global spice trade, which in turn posed the question of what to do with its new-found wealth. Like nouveau riche people everywhere, Manuel built. He commissioned magnificent monasteries, churches, towers and palaces throughout the country, all of which were covered in delicate decorative maritime elements. Although many buildings from this period were destroyed by the huge earthquake in 1755, it is still possible to find architectural relics from Portugal's golden age. These include the "Manueline" windows and doorways on the village churches in Monchique, Luz de Tavira and Alvor, which are covered in ornaments including exotic plants, corals and mooring ropes. The style is truly unique to Portugal.

MOORISH REMNANTS

Citrus, carob and almond trees; irrigation systems; profitable fishing methods; flourishing global trade; religious tolerance and plenty of culture … The Moors brought a great deal to the region during their rule, which began in 711 and lasted until the middle of the 13th century. However, aside from numerous place names (including all those beginning with "Al" or "Gua"), some all-too-perfectly restored fortresses, such as the

TRUE OR FALSE?

SEA AS WARM AS A JACUZZI

If you're headed to the south of Portugal, you probably expect sea temperatures which you could comfortably bathe in. Unfortunately, you are set to be disappointed. This is the Atlantic and it lacks the balmy warmth of the Med. Even in August the water rarely gets much above 20°C. Compared to Croatia, for example, where water temperature regularly hits 27°C, this can feel pretty icy. However, once you've experienced the extreme heat of an Algarve summer, you are likely to see the refreshing cold as a blessing.

A FISHY PEOPLE?

Sardines in the summer, mussels in every month with an "r" in it, and bass, cod, octopus and tuna for the rest of the year. The Algarvios eat seafood like it's going out of fashion (and it kind of is). This is not a place where one says "I don't like fish", and you won't find a menu at a restaurant or local festival without at least a couple of seafood options. It's part of the local culture and quite a few people here still make their living from the sea. Top tip: if you are tempted by more than one fishy option in a restaurant, order the *cataplana*, a selection of dishes which is meant to show off the chef's skills.

one in Silves, and a few archaeological relics, not much is left of their legacy today. The Reconquista (the re-conquest of Iberia) took place in the depths of the Middle Ages, and the Christian knights showed little mercy when it came to the architectural legacy of the Muslim Almohad dynasty. All the region's mosques were replaced with churches in this period, and much of what was left was destroyed in the 1755 earthquake. Most of the existing remnants can be found in the picturesque town of Mértola in Alentejo.

ALL MANNER OF MUSIC

During the summer, live music pumps out of every kind of nightlife establishment. Whether you are into hard rock or chilled-out jazz, you will find a place to fill a few melodious hours at pretty much any time of day or night; for example, the *Café Inglês* (see p. 113) in Silves hosts jazz sessions on Sunday afternoons. Nowadays, several towns also stage fantastic music festivals in their historic centres, with highlights including the annual world music *Festival MED* at the end of June in Loulé and the *Festival F* at the beginning of September in Faro.

And then of course, there is *fado* – the traditional Portuguese song genre that expresses a sense of mournful yearning. Originating from the poor quarters of Lisbon during the 19th century, it is generally accompanied by the distinctively bulbous *guitarra portuguesa* and a "normal" guitar, and is now classed by UNESCO as an Intangible Cultural Heritage. The genre is not actually typical of the Algarve, but can still be heard in many places – for example, at the cultural association *Fado com História* in Tavira.

SALT MOUNTAINS

You will see the gleaming white mountains of salt dotted along the Ria Formosa or in Castro Marim. And you will also find it on sale as a typical Algarve souvenir at any market. But how exactly is salt "harvested"? During the summer, huge basins in the salt marshes are flooded with seawater. As the water evaporates, the salt concentration gradually increases. When the water is channelled into smaller pans, the crystallisation process begins, and the resulting salt is harvested by hand using wooden rakes. At first, this takes the form of valuable *flor de sal*, a particularly grand form of salt that forms every day on the surface of the brine; but after two weeks the rest of the salt is collected. This is an ancient tradition which has not changed much since the Romans used Algarve salt to preserve their fish 2,000 years ago.

TIMES OF CRISIS

The collapse of the construction industry, tax increases, funds from the EU rescue package and severe welfare cutbacks – Portugal went through hard times in the previous decade, the consequences of which are still being felt. Living standards dropped to a low point and the Portuguese were forced to survive on modest means. Due to a lack of investors, new buildings in the Algarve transformed overnight into ruins while other properties remained empty, waiting for prospective buyers. Nonetheless, property prices boomed after the crisis and native Algarvios have found it extremely tough to find places to live. The idea of secure employment and decent wages is still a pipe dream for many people in the region, and often alternative income streams have to be found. Mind you, the Portuguese have a long history of finding a way to get through even the toughest of times.

WINE TASTING

Life isn't easy for the Algarvian wine industry, as it stands in the shadow of Portugal's major wine regions such as Douro, Dão and Alentejo. However, a few wineries are gradually making a name for themselves, and some have even won major awards. You need only visit one of these *quintas* for a tasting to realise how richly deserved their new-found recognition is. The citrus-coloured white wines are soft and fruity; the rosés come with a raspberry aroma; and the reds are full bodied and characterful. The grapes thrive in the sunny maritime climate and the native *terroir*, particularly in the area around Lagoa; but it takes a lot of hard work to produce a good wine. In the past, the wines here were made almost exclusively by cooperatives, and the quality was middling. Now, increasing numbers of small but highly motivated producers are working with dedication and passion and, lo and behold, they have come up with some superb wines.

The methods for gathering salt at Castro Marim haven't changed since Roman times

EATING SHOPPING SPORT

Nightlife in the Praca da Republica in Tavira

EATING & DRINKING

Be it fried, grilled, salted or in kebabs, seafood dominates the Algarve's cuisine.

THE JOY OF EATING

Eating in Portugal is never about just replenishing your energy stocks. Food is celebrated here for its ability to bring friends and families together. At home you may well dash out of the office for a sandwich or force down a soggy salad in the work kitchen, but these modes of eating have no place in the Algarve. The tiny number of fast-food restaurants or chain coffee shops is a reminder that culinary culture here is different; eating takes time and, once you adapt, it is a wonderful thing that it does.

INTERNATIONAL & REGIONAL

A number of restaurants in the region serve French, Italian, Indian or Chinese cuisine. Sometimes you can't beat a decent pizza no matter where in the world you are. For the most part though, the restaurants found in the Algarve serve local dishes, with a heavy focus on seafood and meat, just like across the rest of Portugal. The restaurant business is never easy and not every establishment can keep its head above water, especially if they can only earn money during the summer months. There is also a staggering VAT of up to 23 per cent on food and drink in Portugal. Don't be too surprised if any of the places we recommend here no longer exist by the time of your visit (but don't panic, there will be plenty of other great places).

FOR PENNY PINCHERS

In general, eating out is extremely affordable in Portugal. This obviously does not apply to chic fine-dining restaurants but is true for most simple tascas. Some offer a reasonably priced

Essential flavours of the Algarve: *caldeirada* (left) and grilled sardines (right).

three-course set menu for between 10 and 15 euros, which often includes a drink and an espresso. Ordering a restaurant's daily special – *prato do dia* – normally guarantees you speedy service and the freshest ingredients. If you are not ravenous (Portuguese portions can be enormous), you can often order a half portion – *meia dose* – which in reality equates to 70% of a normal portion.

INSIDER TIP
If you are not crazily hungry...

"NOTHING WITH EYES"

It is not too long ago that only very few chefs in the Algarve could understand why anyone would voluntarily refuse to eat meat or fish. Even today it is fairly common to get fish if you ask for a vegetarian option. But times are slowly changing and thankfully it is increasingly common to see a couple of vegeatrian dishes on a menu. *Happycow.net* has a pretty comprehensive list of veggie and vegan restaurants.

THE TASTE OF THE SEA

But seafood remains the all-time favourite choice. In the Algarve you can eat fish specialities for 15 euros which would cost you two or three times that in the UK. Most fish is served grilled with boiled potatoes and a hunk of lemon – simple but delicious. If you fancy trying something a bit more adventurous, go for a *cataplana*, one of the Algarve's most traditional dishes and presented in a copper pot (which bears more than a passing resemblance to a UFO). In the pot is a rich mixture of different types of fish (and very often mussels too).

MUSSEL TRAINING

Talking of mussels, the area around the Ria Formosa is responsible for almost the entire country's shellfish harvest. From *berbigões* (cockles) to *mexilhões* (mussels) and from *lingueirões* (razor clams) to *ostras* (oysters), this area is a shellfish paradise. *Perceves* (goose barnacles) may look like chicken feet but they taste amazing with a cool beer. Due to the constant battering by the waves and water, harvesting them is very risky, which explains the high prices. In general, shellfish are frequently served as an *entrada* (starter).

NO BREAD – NO MEAL

Before you order a soup or another starter, you will typically be offered a *couvert*, which consists of bread, butter, olives and sometimes a carrot salad with a tasty dressing. Feel free to refuse it if you don't feel very hungry as you do have to pay for it. However, for Portuguese people bread is an integral part of every meal, and refusing the bread may raise a few baffled glances from your fellow diners. With good reason too: dunked in a soup or used to soak up the cooking juice from mussels or a delicious sauce, it will more than earn its modest keep on your table if you give it a chance.

SWEET DELIGHTS

Desserts in the Algarve will also have you reaching for the nearest possible superlative. A *pudim flan* is delicate and delicious enough but most places also offer a *doce da casa* (home-made dessert) to tempt you. These tantalising delicacies are often made from mixing meringues and almonds with figs, citrus fruits and cream.

SÁUDE!

Most restaurants serve *vinho da casa* (house wines), which are mostly from Alentejo and normally represent excellent value. However, it is still worth taking a look at the wine list. A well-chilled *vinho verde* (white wine) is the perfect accompaniment to fish dishes. Whites from the Minho region in Portugal's north are young, light and very fresh. As such they are a world away from some of the reds from the Dão or Douro regions, which (while often fantastic) are decidedly heavier. There is also a growing number of decent Algarvian wines. Port comes exclusively from the Douro region but can act as the perfect introduction or conclusion to any meal.

A NIGHTCAP?

Need a digestif after a heavy meal? With either a *medronho* – schnapps made from the strawberry tree – or a *bagaço* (pomace brandy) you have the choice of excellent local options. After that, you can take the edge off the alcohol with a cup of coffee (*bica*). Alternatively, if you have no fear of a hangover, you can order a *bica com cheirinho* (coffee with "firewater"). At this point it really will be time to get out of the restaurant. *"A conta, se faz favor"* will get you to the business end of the evening, as will making the international sign for "The bill, please". In Portugal, it is unusual for there to be complicated negotiations about who ate what. Either one person pays for the whole table or you split evenly so you can make a quick exit! Don't forget to leave a tip (around 10%) on the table.

Today's Specials

Starters

CENOURAS À ALGARVIA
Carrot salad with garlic and
fresh coriander

SOPA DE PEIXE
Hearty fish soup

SALADA DE POLVO
Octopus salad with onions

Main courses

PEIXE DO DIA
Catch of the day prepared on the grill:
pargo (bream), *espadarte* (swordfish)
or *robalo* (seabass)

SARDINHAS ASSADAS
Grilled sardines with boiled potatoes
and salad (ideally only in summer)

CALDEIRADA
A traditional seafood stew

FRANGO PIRI-PIRI
Grilled chicken in a spicy sauce
(familiar from the one of the UK's
most popular chain restaurants)

Desserts

DOM RODRIGO
Sweet treat made from almonds,
cinnamon and angel hair (sweet threads
of egg boiled in sugar syrup)

TORTA DE ALFARROBA E MEL
Sweet roll made from carob flour,
honey, almonds and eggs

QUEIJO DE FIGO
Not, in fact, cheese – a fig and
almond cake

Drinks

VINHO REGIONAL
Wine from the Algarve

CERVEJA SAGRES
Beer (which is in fact brewed north of
Lisbon, not in Sagres)

MEDRONHO
Digestif made from the fruits of
the strawberry tree

CAFÉ/BICA
Small, strong coffee
(very like an espresso)

SHOPPING

CORKY DESIGN

The bark of the cork oak trees is not only transformed into cork for bottles or floors, but into beautiful accessories. Made of "cork leather", these include glasses cases, belts, bags, umbrellas, hats, sandals, wallets and more. Waterproof, flexible and fire resistant, it has become a great alternative to leather for those who wish to avoid using animal products. Not only that but, when you run a hand over it, you will discover a velvety softness which elevates it above run-of-the-mill cow hide. It's true: cork is the most common, most beautiful and most practical Portuguese export.

NOT IDEAL FOR PLATE SPINNING

If you think Portuguese pottery is just a lot of ancient tiles, then think again. Near Porches, on the N 125, there are several ceramic workshops selling a huge range of products, from beautifully designed plates and bowls to colourful teacups and elegant vases. You can even commission your ceramic item of choice. *Azulejos* are of course available too, as is perhaps the most Portuguese of all pottery … the ceramic sardine!

A UFO FOR YOUR HOUSE

Looking for a bed pan or need some décor for a space-themed party? Then buy yourself your very own *cataplana*: You never know you might even cook with it one day too …

COLOURFUL COCKERELS WHEREVER YOU LOOK

You will see colourfully glazed ceramic cockerels virtually everywhere in the Algarve even though they're an import from Portugal's north. A pilgrim to Santiago de Compostela was accused of theft and brought in front of a judge who happened to be eating

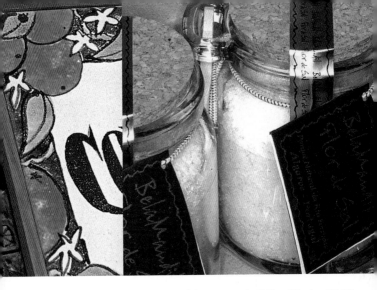

Souvenirs worth buying: ceramics (left) and *flor de sal* (right)

a chicken. The pilgrim pled his innocence and claimed that the cockerel would crow as proof of his lack of pilfering. Improbably, the ex-chicken then made a sound … and a legend was born. The souvenir shop industry has been rubbing its hands ever since.

EXTRA HOT

Are you a fan of spicy food? On the Algarve you can find *piri-piri* (chilli) either dried, as a powder or in sauces – making it ideal for adding some heat to your food.

The strong *medronho* brandy produced and sold mainly in the mountain villages of the Serra de Monchique can also pack quite a bit of heat. *Melosa* (*medronho* with added honey) offers a sweeter alternative.

SWEET-TOOTHED TASTINESS

You can find sweet and fruity cakes made of figs, almonds and honey, and there are also endless varieties of biscuits made with the same ingredients – as well as carob (*alfarroba*) and sweet potato (*batata doce*) – all of which make great souvenirs. Almost every supermarket will have a shelf dedicated to these delicacies.

SALT & SHAKE

Sea salt and the highly prized *flor de sal* from the Algarve's saltworks are sold in attractive little bags all over the region. The salt is often mixed with all kinds of herbs and spices, from thyme to peri-peri and lemon zest. Salt in Loulé's market is very good value (a couple of euros a bag). Light but local and absolutely delicious, it makes an excellent gift for everyone back home.

INSIDER TIP
Souvenirs which will actually get used!

SPORT & ACTIVITIES

From diving and snorkelling to surfing, kayaking and sailing – the Algarve is an ideal choice for watersports enthusiasts.

But there are also lots of things to do on dry land: Portugal's south is famous for its golf courses, and its diverse landscape is ideal for hiking, biking or horse riding.

CYCLING

Although the markings on the 214-km east–west *Ecovia* cycle path are a little faded, it is possible to cycle from the *Cabo de São Vicente* to the Spanish border following the coastline along the way. However, several parts of the route require riding on very busy roads. The historic route followed by the new *Rota Vicentina (en.rotavicentina.com)* long-distance trail is suited to any cyclists, while the *Via Algarviana (www.viaalgarviana.org)* is best attempted by those wanting to recreate Tour de France mountain stages. Unsurprisingly, mountain bikes are a must on the latter route. Guided mountain-bike tours – including from the summit of Mount Fóia down to the coast – are available from *Outdoor Tours (www.outdoor-tours.com)*. If you prefer to pick your own route you can also hire bikes at *Megasport (megasportravel.com/en)* in Loulé or *Abilio Bikes (abiliobikes.com)* in Tavira.

HIKING

There is a surprisingly large selection of beautiful hiking trails, ranging from narrow paths along the clifftops of the rocky Algarve coast or the Costa Vicentina – especially via the well-signposted *Rota Vicentina (en.rotavicentina.com)* hiking trail – to trails among the lagoons of the Ria Formosa and the Ria de Alvor and walking routes through the hills of the hinterland. Here you will find the *Via*

Gain a different perspective by paddling around the cliffs of Ponta da Piedade

Algarviana (www.viaaalgarviana.org) long-distance trail offering 300km of unique walking, as well as a number of smaller circular trails. Whatever route you choose, temperatures will be very hot during the summer, while in spring wildflowers colour the wayside. You can book great guided tours around the west of the Algarve with the superb guide *Nicolau da Costa (tel. 9 67 93 22 06)*. With a background in landscape gardening, a passion for surfing and a penchant for foraging *perceves* (goose barnacle), he is an extremely experienced guide who knows the paths along the west coast like the back of his hand and a knowledgeable and entertaining companion. His smugglers' stories and extremely impressive flora and fauna identification skills mean a walk with Nicolau is never dull.

INSIDER TIP
Nicolau's rugged walking tours

HORSE RIDING

Lusitano horses are a popular choice in the Algarve. Despite being Arab thoroughbreds (famed for their hot-blooded temperament), they are well behaved and easy to control – and also very comfortable to ride. Just about every riding school *(centro hípico)* uses Lusitanos.

Quinta da Saudade (Hack: 35 euros for 1.5 hrs | tel. 9 68 05 40 13 | cavalos quintadasaudade.com) at Guia offers guided horse riding around the Lagoa dos Salgados, including to the beach at Praia Grande near Armação de Pêra or through the dunes. The horses and ponies are very tame and suitable for beginners. The *Horse Shoe Ranch (tel. 2 82 47 13 04 | horseshoeranch.de/ page1_eng/index.php)* in Mexilhoeira Grande offers riding holidays for all levels (715 / 980 euros a week), including full board and accommodation in one of four apartments.

Hiking near Barranco do Velho

KAYAK TRIPS

One of the best water-sport experiences on the Algarve – at least when conditions are good – is to paddle along the rugged rocky coast and explore the golden grottoes of the Ponta da Piedade in Lagos. A guided kayak tour lasts around three hours and costs 30 euros at *Outdoor Tours (Lagos | kayak-lagos.com),* though there are other providers available.

The canals and lagoons of the Ria Formosa are also ideal for exploring by kayak, and you can see plenty of birdlife on the two- or four-hour guided tours run by *Formosamar (bases in Faro and Tavira | formosa mar.com).* Prices start at 35 euros.

PADDLEBOARDING & SURFING

⚐ The best place to ride the waves is the west coast – especially the Praia do Amado, the Praia da Arrifana and the area around Sagres. Windsurfers and kitesurfers love the Meia Praia at Lagos, the beaches around Portimão and the Ilha de Faro. Stand-up paddleboarding is very popular, and during the summer you can see people on their boards all along the south coast. Beware: the Atlantic Ocean can be unpredictable, so if you are inexperienced consider taking a course – e.g. at *Algarve Watersports (algarvewater sports.com)* in Lagos.

ROCK CLIMBING

Unlike many areas of southern Spain, the Algarve is not exactly a paradise for climbers; however, there are crags available on the slopes of the flat Rocha da Pena mountain as well as on the rocky cliffs at Sagres and the Cabo de São Vicente. The climbing scene is still small here, with an informal, low-key atmosphere.

Guided climbing tours and courses for alll levels are available from

Algarve Adventure (HQ: Surfschool Algarve Adventure | Praia de Monte Clérigo bei Aljezur | tel. 9 13 53 33 63 | algarve-adventure.com). Equipment is included and prices start at 60 euros.

RUNNING

Fancy a holiday half marathon? Faro hosts one in March and the Lagos one is in May. There are also a large number of trail-running events each year for those who like their running to be a bit more treacherous. Upcoming events are listed on the *Associação do Atletismo do Algarve website: crono. aaalgarve.org.*

SAILING

The wind conditions at Europe's south-western edge make it an ideal place for sailing. Rainer Klemm and his experienced team offer two-day taster courses from 170 euros on catamarans, dinghies or oppies: *Sailcompany (tel. 9 10 39 37 00 | sailcompany. com)*. This company based on the Meia Praia at Lagos is a member of the Association of Windsurfing and Water Sports Schools (VDWS), which means that the sailing certificates you can obtain here are recognised internationally. There is also a private hour-long taster course costing 50 euros (for two people) that will take you along the Lagos coastline with its many grottoes.

SCUBA DIVING

The diversity of fish species – particularly in Sagres – is huge and visibility is generally very good unless you catch an unfavourable current. The water can be very cold, so thick wetsuits are advisable. A number of shipwrecks lie off the coast at Portimão and it is possible to visit them on your dives; the *Subnauta (www.subnauta. pt)* diving school is the place to go if you want to explore these relics of sea voyages past. In Sagres, the diving school *Divers Cape (www.diverscape. net)* takes you to the best spots. If you want to dive off the coast of Lagos, John, Elmar and the team at *Blue Ocean Divers (http://blue-ocean-divers. eu)* are excellent. All diving schools offer beginners' courses for those wanting to dip their toe (and quite a lot more besides) into the world of scuba diving. If you enjoy these taster sessions, you can carry on and get your PADI certificate allowing you in the future to dive without an instructor being present. It's a ticket to a whole new underwater world.

Paddleboarding is all the rage

REGIONAL OVERVIEW

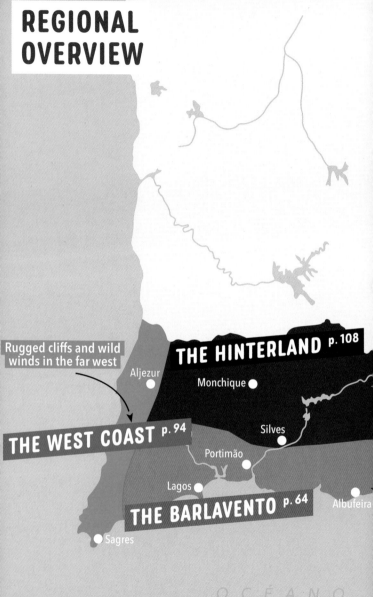

Rugged cliffs and wild winds in the far west

THE HINTERLAND p. 108

Aljezur

Monchique

Silves

THE WEST COAST p. 94

Portimão

Lagos

Albufeira

THE BARLAVENTO p. 64

Sagres

OCÉANO

15 km
9.32 mi

Mountain scenery and traditional towns

THE SOTAVENTO p. 38

Alcoutim

ESPAÑA

Río Guadiana

Río Guadiana

Vila Real de
Santo Antonio

Loulé

Tavira

Estói

Lagoons, salt flats and
vast sandy beaches

Faro

Olhão

Party by night,
sunbathe in the rocky
coves by day

ATLANTICO

THE SOTAVENTO

BEAUTIFUL BEACHES & SCINTILLATING CITIES

What makes the Algarve such a great place to visit is its rich contrasts. A little to the east of Faro is the start of the sandy part of the Algarve coast. From here to the Rio Guadiana on the Spanish border there is not a rocky cove to be seen; the high cliffs are replaced by glorious, long sandy beaches, which rarely feel crowded, even in summer.

Many of these beaches are located on the islands of the Ria Formosa conservation area – a set of lagoons whose salt flats, flocks

Sand and sea in the Ria Formosa National Park at Tavira

of flamingos and shellfish of every variety make for a stunning landscape and rich culture. Some of the Algarve's most exciting towns and cities were founded hundreds of years ago on the shores of the Ria Formosa. Take some time to explore them; each has its own special character. You can find solitude and wilderness in the hilly hinterland to the east. In fact, if you are looking for peace and quiet on your holiday, then the eastern end of the Algarve is the place to be.

THE SOTAVENTO

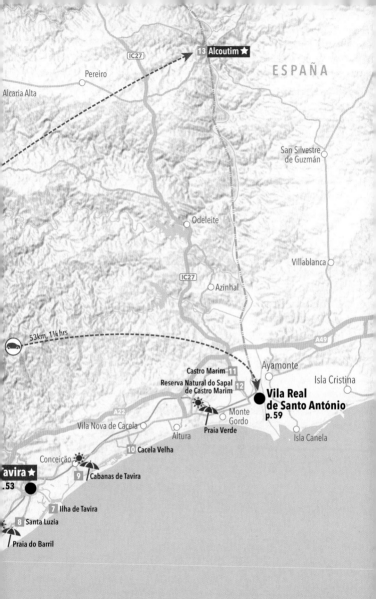

IC27

Pereiro

Alcaria Alta

13 Alcoutim ★

ESPAÑA

San Silvestre
de Guzmán

Odeleite

Villablanca

IC27

Azinhal

A49

53km, 1¼ hrs

Ayamonte

Isla Cristina

Castro Marim 11

Reserva Natural do Sapal
de Castro Marim 12

Vila Real
de Santo António
p.59

Monte
Gordo

Praia Verde

A22

Vila Nova de Cacela

Altura

Isla Canela

10 Cacela Velha

Conceição

9 Cabanas de Tavira

avira ★
.53

7 Ilha de Tavira

8 Santa Luzia

Praia do Barril

OCEANO ATLÂNTICO

4 km
2.49 mi

FARO

(📖 M7–8) **If the only place you visit in Faro is its airport, you are missing out. It's worth spending some time in the Algarve's capital to visit its charming old town, *Vila-Adentro*. But there is much more to this small city than a few pretty old buildings.**

Faro (pop. 47,000) is a breath of fresh air, primarily because it is just an ordinary city, with a university, shopping precincts, industrial estates and, above all, lots of Portuguese people who live, study, shop and work here. You might find a few tourists in the old town, but the atmosphere is different to other towns in the Algarve, partly thanks to the alternative student bar scene. Faro also has plenty of culture on offer, with a theatre, museums, churches and a fascinating history.

The port city was called Ossonoba by the Romans, while the Moors knew it as Harúm. Faro was the last fortress held by the Moors in Portugal before King Alfonso III "reconquered" it in 1249. After the earthquake in 1755 destroyed large parts of Lagos, the Algarve's regional administration was moved from there to Faro, at which point the city began to develop into the country's southern capital.

SIGHTSEEING

VILA-ADENTRO (OLD TOWN) ★

Faro's historic centre is supremely picturesque, and its cosy cobbled streets, the beautiful cathedral precinct of the Largo da Sé and the well-preserved city walls more than make up for the many less attractive parts of town. The *Cidade Velha* is accessed through one of the city gates, the grandest of which is the 18th-century *Arco da Vila* by the *Jardim Manuel Bivar*. The statue above the arch is of the city's patron saint Thomas Aquinas. In spring storks take up residence here by building nests in the bell tower. Parts of the *Arco do Repouso* (Gate of Rest) date back to the 13th century – this is also where Alfonso III is reputed to have recovered after his battle against the Moors. The conquest of the city is depicted on *azulejo* tiles next to the city gate. The 17th-century *Arco da Porta Nova* leads onto a small promenade that runs parallel to the railway and the Ria Formosa behind it.

SÉ

Cameras at the ready! With its elongated, whitewashed bishop's palace (the *Paço Episcopal*), its orange trees and especially the cathedral, the Largo da Sé forms a harmonious and highly photogenic ensemble in the heart of the old town. This site was the location of the forum during Roman times; later on, the Visigoths founded a Christian church here before the Moors came and converted it into a mosque. After the Reconquista, construction of a new Christian place of worship was begun on top of all these ruins in 1251, but the form of the church was modified in response to an attack by pirates and the 1755 earthquake. Today it features an exciting mix of styles, from the Gothic bell tower (from the top there are amazing

views over the old town and the Ria Formosa) to the lavishly painted Baroque organ installed by the

INSIDER TIP
Far reaching views over Faro

German organ builder Arp Schnitger in 1716. There is a *museum containing sacred art* within the Sé, and you can also visit a small bone chapel in the inner courtyard. *Mon–Fri 10am–6.30pm (winter 10am–6pm), Sat 9.30am–1pm | admission 3.50 euros*

MUSEU MUNICIPAL

It is worth visiting the city museum for the stunning Renaissance building alone – the 16th-century former ☂ *Convento Nossa Senhora da Assunção*, with its two-storey cloister and beautiful garden. But don't forget

Take in the view from the cathedral bell tower

to check out the exhibitions too, which range from fascinating Roman, Visigoth and Moorish artefacts to a gallery filled with works by local Renaissance and Baroque artists. *Tue–Fri 10am–6pm (summer 10am–7pm), Sat/Sun 10.30am–5pm (summer 11.30am–6pm) | admission 2 euros | Sun until 2.30pm (summer 3.30pm) admission free | Praça Alfonso III 14 | FB: museumunicipaldefaro*

IGREJA DE SÃO FRANCISCO

Perhaps due to its unremarkable exterior, barely anyone visits this 17th-century monastic church. However, there are few better examples of why not to judge a building by its cover than this little gem. The interior positively drips with stunning *azulejos* and golden woodcuts. Don't just peek in either, the further inside you go, the more colourful it becomes. *Mon–Fri 8am–noon and 5.30–7.30pm | admission 1 euro | Largo de São Francisco 51*

CENTRO CIÊNCIA VIVA DO ALGARVE

In 1910, when the first electric streetlights lit up Faro's narrow streets, a small power station was built on the edge of the Rio Formosa. Today, it has been transformed into an interactive science museum which will help you to understand how the Ria Formosa was formed and will introduce you to many of the flora and fauna which populate it today. However, its past life as a power station has not been com-

A bit gruesome: Capela dos Ossos

pletely erased. In the garden, a small wind and tidal power station creates modern green energy. Do not miss the chance to come in the hours of darkness (registration is necessary). Once the sun goes down, the museum sets up a telescope in the garden which provides glorious views of the stars over the Algarve. *Tue–Sun 10am–6pm | admission 4 euros (children 2 euros) | Rua Comandante Francisco Manuel | ccvalg.pt*

INSIDER TIP
Stargaze

IGREJA NOSSA SENHORA DO CARMO

The ossuary chapel *(Capela dos Ossos)*, built in 1816 in the garden of the Carmelite church, displays this rather ominous warning above its entrance: "Take heed for you too will end up like this one day". The skulls and bones come from over 1,200 monks who belonged to the order. The church itself is decorated much more cheerfully in a Baroque style. Built in the 18th century, it is lavishly decorated with *talha dourada*, or gilded woodcarvings. *Mon–Fri 10am–1pm and 2–5pm (summer until 6pm), Sat 9am–1pm | admission 2 euros | Largo do Carmo*

JARDIM DA ALAMEDA JOÃO DE DEUS

Boisterous peacocks parade around among huge centuries-old trees while parents drink coffee at the *quiosque* and their children charge around the playground. Faro's largest city park is not only grand in scale, at its southern end it also houses an imposing old slaughterhouse decorated with stunning neo-Moorish arches. Fortunately, it's a more peaceful place today, as this bright orange building was converted into the city library in 2001. Shhh…. *Park daily 7.30am–8.30pm (winter 7.30am–6.30pm) | Rua da Polícia da Segurança Pública*

INSIDER TIP
A building that belongs in the Arabian Nights

EATING & DRINKING

A VENDA

You will notice right away that this small and friendly tapas bar is run by young people, even though the decor and the crockery are more reminiscent of your grandma's front room. The dishes are quirky, creative, fresh and well seasoned, and this place is also a paradise for vegetarians. *Closed Sun | Rua do Compromisso 60 | tel. 2 89 82 55 00 | FB: avendafaro | €*

CAFÉ ALIANÇA

Founded in 1908, this old school café may be great to look at from the outside (and to take photos of) but it is even better inside. Rejuvenated in 2016, it now serves more than just coffee and has become one of the best *cervejarias* in town. Alongside your beer, you can also order hearty portions of *petiscos* (tapas) or larger, more extravagant Algarve dishes such as *cataplana* or tuna steak. *Daily | Rua D Francisco Gomes 7 | tel. 2 89 82 37 63 | www.cafealianca.pt | €€*

FAZ GOSTOS

If you want to eat seriously well and in an unusual yet cosy atmosphere, then this gourmet restaurant in the old town should be your first port of call. The exquisite creations prepared here using typical Portuguese ingredients are surprisingly affordable. The desserts are divine and none more so than the re-creation of a land of milk and honey with filo pastry, goat's cheese, nuts and honey. *Closed Sun | Rua do Castelo 13 | tel. 2 89 87 84 22 | fazgostos.com | €€€*

PIGS & COWS

This young, stylish spot offers superb world food (not limited to pork and beef) in a brilliantly designed space. The dishes are changed regularly according to what is in season and how the chefs feel, but often with an Asian twist. *Tue–Sun 6.30–10pm | Rua Batista Lopes 57 | tel. 9 66 09 68 50 | pigsandcowsalgarve.com | €€*

SHOPPING

Faro's pedestrian zone on *Rua Dom Francisco Gomes* and the surrounding streets offer everything that shoppers could possibly desire. You can find fruit, vegetables and a supermarket at the *market hall (Largo Dr Francisco Sa Carneiro)*. And if you love shopping malls, there are a couple of heavy hitters on the outskirts of Faro: the 🌲 *Forum Algarve (www.forumalgarve. net)* is located outside the city centre, while a heady combination of 🌲 IKEA, designer outlets and a more standard mall is found on the A 22 towards Loulé.

SPORT & ACTIVITIES

It's hard to get bored in Faro with the amazing Ria Formosa on your doorstep. A number of providers offer boat tours through the channels of this lagoon landscape – or for an even more impressive introduction to this conservation area, try a guided kayak tour. If you are interested in the birdlife on the Ria then you can find some great birdwatching spots in the area around Ludo, to the west of the airport. For all these activities it is worth using the eco-tourism agency *Formosamar (formosamar.com)*, based at the marina.

INSIDER TIP
Paddle through lagoons and canals

BEACHES

Faro's main beach, the *Praia de Faro* on the Ilha de Faro is 10km long. In the 1970s a building spree took place here and house after house sprung up on the dunes and the area is heavily built up. You can find parking and a number of bars close to the access road (which runs past the airport and then over a bridge towards the Ria); however, parking spaces become very scarce during the summer, when half of Faro's population decamps onto the Ilha. The further west you go from the city, the calmer (and more exclusive) the beaches get. The rich and famous tend to hang out in the area around Gigi's beach bar at the 🌴 *Quinta do Lago*. The sand here may stretch for miles in all directions allowing you to

Bags of atmosphere: evening street scene in Faro's old town

contemplate the infinite possibilities of life, the universe and beyond, but the prices in the bar will bring you back to earth with a crash.

WELLNESS

Magic Spa (en.magicspa-store.com/pestana-pousada-estoi) in the *Palácio de Estoí* (see p. 48) is not the cheapest place but its gorgeous setting and excellent attention to detail mean it can justify its sporty prices. You don't need to be a hotel guest to book a massage or to use the sauna and pool.

NIGHTLIFE

There is no shortage of nightlife in Faro, especially in the streets to the north of the marina where you will find countless bars and pubs. Many

offer live music during the evening, such as *Bar CheSsenta (Mon–Sat 6pm–4am | Rua do Prior 24 | FB: bar.chessenta)*, which incidentally also serves

INSIDER TIP
Cuban cocktails

very good "mojitos Cubanos". Talking of cocktails, *Columbus Bar (daily noon–4am | Praça Dom Francisco Gomes 13 | barcolumbus.pt)* may look posh from the outside but its prices are fair and the guys behind the bar are veritable magicians of mixology. *O Castelo (daily 10.30am–4am, closed Tue in the winter | Rua do Castelo 11 | FB: OCastelo.CidadeVelha)*, by the walls of the old town, has a varied programme of music and cultural events, ranging from fado, tango and jazz to raucous DJ sets. Its lounge-style terrace overlooking the *ria* is a great place to watch the sun go down.

AROUND FARO

1 ILHA DESERTA

7km south of Faro / 15 mins by boat

The boat trip out to the barrier island *Ilha da Barreta* is a unique experience. The island is uninhabited and has no groundwater, which is why it came to be known as the "desert island", or Ilha Deserta. You can dine all year round here at the fantastic and energy self-sufficient beach restaurant *Estaminé* (tel. 9 17 81 18 56 | ilha-deserta.com | €€€) (booking essential). Afterwards, there are 7km of empty beach waiting for you, or you can take a stroll through the dunes along the 2-km wooden walkway to the *Cabo de Santa Maria*, with its bizarre array of driftwood and signposts. *M–N8*

> **INSIDER TIP**
> **Pathway to Portugal's southernmost point**

2 ALMANCIL

13km northwest of Faro / 20 mins by car on the IC 4/N 125

This sprawling town spread out along the busy N 125 road doesn't have a huge amount to offer. There are a few cafés and restaurants that are occasionally frequented by wealthy holidaymakers (chiefly golfers) from the neighbouring *Vale do Lobo* and *Quinta do Lago* luxury resorts who are in search of a little authentic Portuguese flair. As a result, it does not feature on many itineraries. However, at the eastern end of the town there is a breathtaking church that you shouldn't miss under any circumstances, even if you're not really into churches. The small baroque church ★ ▐ *Igreja de São Lourenço* (Mon 3–6pm, Tue–Sat 10am–1pm and 3–6pm (winter until 5pm) | admission 2 euros | Rua da Igreja) is unique in Portugal: its interior is entirely clad in stunning blue and white *azulejos*. How did a small town like this end up with such a special place of worship? It was financed by the wealthy landowners of the region in order to fulfil a vow made in 1722, which was a particularly dry year. The crops were threatening to fail, so prayers were sent up for water. It rained – and in 1730 the church was completed. *L7*

3 ESTÓI & MILREU

10km north of Faro / 15 mins by car on the N 2

The highlight of the delightfully relaxed village of Estói (pop. 3,600) is

The tiles in the Igreja de São Lourenço create a stunning blue and white display

the little Belle Epoque palace, the *Palácio de Estói (Rua de São José 13)* and its beautiful garden. The splendid Rococo palace once played host to Napoleon Bonaparte's emissaries when they visited the region, and today houses a grand *pousada* (small hotel). ☛ Don't worry though, you don't need to fork out for a room to visit the palace's grand salons and chapel, as non-guests can access the gardens and the ground floor. In the park, make sure you check out the sculpture of Venus housed in a "cave" under the steps – three naked goddesses appear to be emerging from a bath in the small fountain.

One kilometre further south, at ★ *Milreu (▥ M7)*, archaeologists unearthed an incredible discovery at the end of the 19th century: a Roman villa dating from the first century CE, which had been continually expanded until the fourth century and featured its own temple. A few mosaics with fish and dolphin motifs have been preserved, and a visit to the excavation site and museum *(Tue–Sun 9.30am–1pm and 2-5pm, summer 10.30am–1pm, 2-6.30pm) | admission 2 euros)* will help you to picture the expansive living quarters and baths. ▥ N7

OLHÃO

(▥ N7) **You will fall in love with the rather idiosyncratic, yet refreshingly tourist-free town of ★ Olhão (pop. 15,000) on the Ria Formosa the moment you arrive. The labyrinthine streets of the old town wind their way through tiny, idyllic *praças* and past square white houses, while enormous market halls house countless fish stalls; in the harbour you can see the proof that there are still people here who make their living from fishing.**

It's true, the town also has some ugly parts – the blocks of flats in the outer suburbs are rather depressing, and the fish-processing factories to the east of the port are not particularly pleasant to look at either. But when you take a stroll along the lively waterfront promenade with its many restaurants filling the air with the scent of grilled fish, and take in the "real" Algarvian way of life, then your initial enthusiasm for this place will be confirmed.

SIGHTSEEING

IGREJA NOSSA SENHORA DO ROSÁRIO

The best feature of this 18th-century parish church is the fact that you can climb the tower to get an incredible view over the square white houses of the old town with the Ria Formosa in the background. The architecture of these cubic buildings with their flat, terraced roofs is unique in Portugal. Copied by the town's fishermen from buildings they had seen in North Africa, they are slightly reminiscent of the area's Moorish past. The candles in the adjoining *Capela do Senhor dos Aflitos* are lit to ensure the safe return of the fishermen. *Tue–Sat 10am–12.30pm, 3–6.30pm (Sat 10am–12.30pm, 4–6.30pm), Sun 9am–noon | ascent of the tower 1 euro | Praça da Restauração*

MUSEU MUNICIPAL

This small but perfectly formed municipal museum is housed in a building that was formerly home to the local fishermen's fraternity – the late 18th-century *Casa do Compromisso*

Stock up on fresh provisions in the market hall

Marítimo. Alongside displays of archaeological artefacts, it hosts a programme of changing exhibitions on Olhão's cultural history. *Tue-Sat 10am-12.30pm and 2-5.30pm | admission free | Praça da Restauração*

QUINTA DE MARIM

At the eastern end of the town, next to a saltworks, you can find the start of a wonderful natural reserve in which a worthwhile circular trail (4-5km) will introduce you to the beauty of the Ria Formosa lagoon landscape with all its plants and birdlife (keep an eye out for flamingos and storks). The *tide mill* is an interesting feature, and both here and at the *visitor centre* you can learn about the natural habitat of the Ria. *Visitor centre open Mon-Fri 9am-12.30pm and 2-6pm | admission 2.70 euros | Av. Parque Natural Ria Formosa*

CASA JOÃO LÚCIO 🐷

Not a bad gaff! This eccentric "chalet" rises out of the northern edge of the Quinta de Marim. It was built as a weekend retreat by the local poet João Lúcio Pereira (1880-1918), and every staircase, wall and shape within was carefully chosen to fit his eccentric supernatural belief system. Today it houses a small museum with changing exhibitions. *Mon-Fri 9am-12.30pm and 2-5.30pm | admission free*

EATING & DRINKING

You can find numerous restaurants along the shoreline promenade Avenida 5 de Outubro, all offering superb grilled fish. *O Bote (no. 122 | closed Sun. | tel. 2 89 72 11 83 | €€)* has a particularly traditional feel, while *Pitéu da Baixa Mar (closed Mon | no. 18 | tel. 2 89 70 57 49 | €)* serves good food at a reasonable price. And if you want a change from traditional Portuguese food, *Pizza na Pedra (daily | no. 50 | tel. 2 89 70 24 44 | pizzapedra.com | €€)* serves (as the name suggest) excellent pizza. Enjoy!

VAI E VOLTA

José and Maria João's rodizio barbecue restaurant has been packing in a huge number of punters for years. Unlike most Brazilian barbecues in other parts of the world, the emphasis here is on excellent fish. There is no need to pick things from a menu – waiters bring around different kinds of fish until you can't take any more. It's a great concept if you like fish (and don't mind a bit of a queue – they don't take reservations) *Tue-Sun, only lunch | Largo do Grémio 2 | vaievolta. pt | €*

SHOPPING

The bustling *market halls (Mon-Sat 7am-1pm | Av. 5 de Outoubro)* are one of the highlights of Olhão. You won't find a bigger fish market anywhere on the Algarve and the fruit and veg is great too. There is also a weekly market every Saturday on the square by the market halls, while some nice little shops can be found on the pedestrianised *Rua do Comércio. Algarve Outlet (N 125 No. 100, algarveoutlet. pt)* pulls in shoppers with its large

Island paradise: you'll have the beach to yourself on the Ilha da Culatra

supermarket, big chain stores, restaurants and cinema.

SPORT & ACTIVITIES

What could be better while in Olhão than a visit to the lagoon? A great way to get to know this magical (but fragile) habitat is to take a boat trip with ☎ *Sabino Boattours (tel. 9 15 66 18 60 | sabinoboattours.com)*. The crew know the region like the back of their hands and can identify all the local birds as well as explain how to harvest mussels and oysters. They will even be able to point out the kind of grasses and reeds most enjoyed by seahorses. The five-hour tour includes a delicious lunch.

AROUND OLHÃO

4 CULATRA ★
3km from Olhão / 30 mins by ferry to Culatra

If you want to get to Olhão's nearest beaches, then you first need to take a fabulous boat trip. On the quay at the eastern end of the shoreline promenade you will find ferries (for timetables go to olhao.web.pt/horari-obarcos.htm) and pleasure boats that will take you across the Ria Formosa to the offshore dune islands of *Armona* and *Culatra (▥ O7–8)*. A few hundred people live here, and most of them work as fishermen or mussel pickers. You won't find any cars here: this is a place to enjoy glorious beaches and plenty of delicious fresh seafood in one of the few restaurants. The atmosphere is very friendly all over the islands. The fishing harbour in the main resort, *Culatra*, is especially picturesque. The western edge of the island is called *Ilha do Farol* ("lighthouse island") thanks to the imposing lighthouse built here in 1851. This red and white beauty can be visited on Wednesday afternoons (2–5pm). It might be a long way up but the view from the top is outstanding.

INSIDER TIP
222 steps to stunning views

⑤ FUSETA

12km east of Olhão/ 20 mins by car on the N 125

In this small coastal resort (pop. 1,900) most people set course straight for the jetty, from where it's a five-minute trip across the Ria Formosa to *Ilha de Fuseta* with its wonderful sandy beach. The Ilha de Fuseta is actually an extension to the Ilha da Armona, and theoretically you can walk all the way there along the beach (which is surprisingly empty, even in summer). Back on the mainland, you will find a few bars on the waterfront, and delicious grilled fish is available at *Casa Corvo (closed Mon | Largo 1° de Maio 1 | tel. 9 14 13 00 29 | €)* near the market hall. Make sure you pay a visit to the church on the outskirts of the village; from its elevated forecourt you can enjoy a beautiful view over Fuseta's white roofs and the Ria. ◫ 07

⑥ MONCARAPACHO

13km north of Olhão / 25 mins by car to Cerro da Cabeça

If you feel the need for something a bit hillier while staying on this extremely flat bit of coast, the *Cerro da Cabeça* is the place to head. Rising up behind the village of Moncarapacho, its harsh landscape is pockmarked by small craters and deep sinkholes. There is a good circular walk (approx. 7km) but not many waymarkers, so keep an eye out. On the way you will see what kind of vegetation survives in this harsh landscape before scrambling up to the highest point from which you get an excellent view over the surrounding region and the Ria Formosa. ◫ 06–7

TAVIRA

(◫ P6) ★ **Tavira is unquestionably the most beautiful town on the Ria Formosa. Its location on the gently flowing Rio Gilão, its many beautiful bridges and churches, and the white houses with their hipped roofs that are so typical of Tavira all lend the town a picturesque air.**

In the past, the inhabitants mainly earned their living from salt production and fishing, and in the 15th century the port was an important trading post with North Africa. However, Portugal's African colonial possessions were not held for long and in time the port silted up. When the tuna fish also disappeared in the 20th century, Tavira sank into a

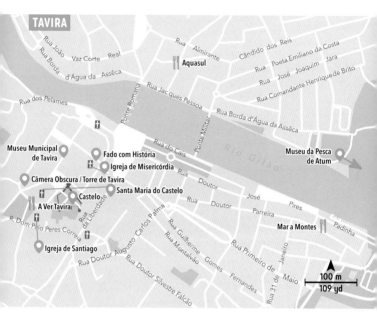

slumber from which it has only recently been awakened by the tourist industry.

Take your time exploring Tavira (pop. 15,000) on both sides of its river. Potter around the narrow, hilly streets and soak up the town's quiet charm. Wander from one church to the next – there are more than 20 here altogether. Or simply sit back on the beautiful shoreline promenade, under the shade of a palm tree in the idyllic *Jardim Público* next to the old market hall, or in one of the inviting street cafés on the *Praça da República*, and watch the world go by.

And should the need to see the sea grow too strong, jump on a ferry and head out to the *Ilha de Tavira*, which is just a few minutes away.

SIGHTSEEING

CHURCHES ON THE FORTRESS HILL

There is no shortage of churches and chapels in Tavira. However, not all 21 of them are accessible to the public and some are more worth visiting than others. Whatever you do, don't miss the churches around the castle. The harmonious, triple-aisled *Santa Maria do Castelo (Mon-Fri 10am-1pm and 2-5pm (summer until 9.30pm) Sat 10am-1pm (summer 2-5pm) | admission 2.50 euros | ☛ combined ticket with the Misericórdia Church 4 euros)* can be spotted from a distance thanks to the enormous clock face on its tower, as well as its elevated position next to the castle. This formerly Gothic church was built on the site of the Moorish mosque during the 13th century, in the wake of the Reconquista, and was given a Manueline extension later on. The 1755 earthquake left its mark but the Gothic entrance portal managed to survive. A second entrance leads to an *exhibition* of sacred art.

From here it's just a short walk to the understated *Igreja de Santiago (irregular opening times | admission free)* which also dates back to the 13th century. The medallion above the main entrance is interesting in that it depicts São Tiago – St James – on horseback. It is a nod to the fact that the knights of the Order of Santiago, who vanquished the Moors during the conquest of the city in 1242, had occupied the Castelo after the Reconquista. Inside the church there are some precious artworks by Portuguese painters that date from the 15th to 18th centuries.

The lavishly decorated *Igreja da Misericórdia (Mon 9.30am–noon and 2–5pm, Tue-Sat 9.30am–1pm and 2–6pm (Sun also in summer) | admission 2.50 euros, combined ticket (see above) 4 euros)* mainly offers 16th-century features: blue and white Rococo *azulejos*, an enormous gilded main altar, and a well-preserved 18th-century cabinet organ balanced on a pedestal that looks as if it is made of marble, but is in fact wooden. You can also visit the vestry and its neighbouring rooms. Make sure you take a look at the Renaissance entrance portal, on which the Mother of God is sheltered by a canopy of stone and flanked by the coats of arms of both Portugal and Tavira.

CASTELO 🐗

Only a few bits of wall from the former Moorish fortress have survived, but the Castelo with its beautifully maintained small garden is still one of the most enchanting places in Tavira. If you have a head for heights, climb up the walls and enjoy the view over the town and the river. *In winter, daily 9am–5pm, in summer Mon-Fri 8am–7pm, Sat/Sun 10am–7pm | admission free*

CAMERA OBSCURA / TORRE DE TAVIRA 👀

A short lesson on optics. Housed in the old water tower, the camera obscura projects live images of Tavira onto a large screen with its lens system. You get a view of the town right across to the salt marshes with a guide telling you all about what you see, including the typical hipped roofs of the old town. *Mon-Fri 10am–4/5pm, summer also Sat 10am–1pm | admission 4 euros, children 2 euros | Calçada da Galeria 12 | torredetavira.com*

MUSEU MUNICIPAL DE TAVIRA

The town museum occupies a number of sites throughout the town, including two chapels and a former water-pumping station. The former residence of the *Palácio da Galeria (Calçada da Galeria)* is worth visiting on architectural grounds alone, but it also hosts a changing programme of exhibitions as well as a display of Phoenician artefacts in the atrium. The museum's *Núcleo Islâmico (Praça da Républica)* branch is devoted entirely to archaeology, and is located on the

Tavira: the 17th-century Ponte Romana spans the Rio Gilão with its seven arches

site where remnants of the 12th-century Moorish city wall and a unique vase – the

INSIDER TIP
Fabulous find

so-called "Vaso de Tavira" – was unearthed in 1996. This unique earthenware pot dates back to the 11th century and its rim is decorated with miniature soldiers, musicians and animals – an incredible find indeed. *Both museums Tue–Sat 9.15am–4.30pm | admission 2 euros, combined ticket 3 euros | museumunicipaldetavira.cm-tavira.pt*

FADO COM HISTÓRIA

Content warning: nostalgic music and a sense of melancholy. This ambitious cultural association presents half-hourly *fado* performances, as well as occasional evening concerts in the *Igreja da Misericórdia* next door. Visitors are first shown a ten-minute film explaining the history and special features of this melancholic Portuguese genre, before experiencing the passion of its singers and guitarists in a live concert *Mon–Sat 11.15am, 12.15pm, 3.15pm, 4.15pm, 5.15pm | admission 5 euros | Rua Damião Augusto de Brito Vasconcelos 4 | fadocomhistoria. wixsite.com/fado*

MUSEU DA PESCA DE ATUM 🐟

Once the biggest tuna-fishing base in the Algarve, today hotel guests occupy the rooms where fishermen used to spend their summers. Decades of overfishing brought an end to the industry here in the 1970s but the small museum explains how these silvery-blue kings and queens of the sea used to be caught and gives advice on how to cook them too. *Daily 8am–7pm (winter 8am–5pm) | free admission | Hotel Vila Galé Albacora, Quatro Águas*

EATING & DRINKING

AQUASUL
This colourful and playful restaurant situated in the old town on the north bank of the Rio Gilão is decorated with beautiful mosaics – but the art isn't limited to the venue's many nooks and crannies (both inside and on the promenade), as the Italian-influenced dishes on the varied menu are also highly creative. Booking essential. *Closed Sun, Mon, closed lunchtime | Rua Doutor Augusto Silva Carvalho 11 | tel. 2 81 32 51 66 | FB: restaquasul | €€*

A VER TAVIRA
Of course, when you come here, you're partly paying for the hilltop location and the amazing views over the town from the terrace – but it is worth it for the food too, with tasty fare such as deep-fried avocado and artfully marinated tuna. *Daily (closed Mon in winter) | Calçada da Galeria 13 | tel. 2 81 38 13 63 | avertavira.com | €€–€€€*

MAR A MONTES
This pleasant *petiscaria* next to the waterfront has a cosy, maritime feel, and offers a varied menu of small but tasty, tapas dishes (mainly seafood-based), as well as craft beers and a huge wine selection. Live bands play here on weekend evenings. *Closed Sat lunch and Sun | Rua José Pires Padinha 164 | tel. 9 14 72 20 89 | FB: maramontespetiscaria | €*

NIGHTLIFE

In the summer, there are many festivals and concerts near the old market hall and on the Praça da República. In the winter, people prefer to meet up in the cafés in the old town, e.g. *Sitio (closed Sun | Largo do Trem 28)* or the *Irish Pub Reilley's (Rua do Poeta Emiliano da Costa | FB: irishpubtavira)*, where bands play every evening. Thanks to *Echo (Fri/Sat 11pm–6am | Av. dos Descobrimentos | FB: echotavira)* there is also a club where you can dance until dawn.

AROUND TAVIRA

🟦 ILHA DE TAVIRA
3km from Tavira / 20 mins by ferry
The 10km-long dunes here are a rare beauty. Boats set sail all year round from the *Quatro Águas* station, just outside Tavira, while in summer passengers usually board near Tavira's former indoor market hall. Tavira island has a row of restaurants and a camping site. Unfortunately, the island can be plagued by mosquitoes in the summer but it is still worth visiting for the incredible beach. *📖 O–P 6–7*

Spruced up:
white and blue tones in Cacela Velha

8 SANTA LUZIA

4km southwest of Tavira / 8 mins by car on the M 515

Santa Luzia is best known for octopus fishing and the harbour promenade with views of the fishing boats is delightful. If you drive another 2km to the *Pedras d'el Rei* holiday resort, then either take a tram or walk along the causeway over the Ria Formosa and through the dunes (1.5km), you will get to the wonderful 🏖 *Praia do Barril* on the Ilha de Tavira. This beach was also once the site of a tuna-fishing station, and its buildings are now home to a number of cafés and restaurants such as the relaxed *Barril Beach Café (€)* The best thing here is, however, the anchor cemetery. These anchors were formerly used to fix fishing nets in place in the sea. 📖 *P7*

> **INSIDER TIP**
> Photoshoot in an anchor cemetery

9 CABANAS DE TAVIRA

8km to the east of Tavira / 10 mins by car on the N 125

This place (pop. 1,100) may at first sight seem rather unimpressive. However, first impressions can be deceiving. It is in fact the boarding point for a ferry service sailing through the lagoon to the long stretch of beautiful beach at 🏖 *Praia de Cabanas*. It's a true paradise: on one side you can swim in the warm lagoon water, on the other in the cooler seawater. The resort itself has a welcoming promenade with plenty of (fish) restaurants. Probably the best ice cream in the Algarve can be tasted at *Delizia (Av. da Ria Formosa | deliziagelatonatural.*

INSIDER TIP
Time for an ice cream

com) with unusual flavours such as honey, ginger, thyme, carob or fig – in other words: all the typical Algarve flavours. *P6*

⑩ CACELA VELHA

12km east of Tavira / 15 mins by car on the N 125

A few dozen houses and a small harbour fort dating back to the 12th century, this place has an idyllic setting above the Ria lagoon. Enjoy the views at the esplanade in front of the church, which is also worth a visit. The *village cemetery* is typical of the Algarve region, with coffin drawers stacked one on top of the other. A small and pleasant footpath leads across the sand (and is best used during low tide) to the village of *Fábrica*, 1.5km to the west (also accessible by car). From here (they offer the same service in Cacela Velha too), the fishermen will ferry you across to the beach on the offshore strips of dunes in their small boats. *Q6*

VILA REAL DE SANTO ANTÓNIO

(R5–6) **As you wander through this chic grid-planned town located on the Rio Guadiana by the Spanish border, you will immediately notice that the atmosphere here is different to other holiday resorts.**

Vila Real is a typical border town, and Spanish people come here to do their shopping, while day-trippers visit to see the town that was personally designed in the 18th century by the Marquês de Pombal, Prime Minister of Portugal.

The king at the time was unhappy that the border region was so sparsely populated, and he also wanted to supervise the trade of goods across the Rio Guadiana and the fishing industry in Monte Gordo after the 1755 earthquake. As a result, over the course of five months in 1774, he erected this "Royal City" on the site of the small fishing village of Santo António de Avelinha. His supervision plan didn't quite work out as intended: the relatively well-off fishermen in nearby Monte Gordo refused to move and decided instead to join with Spain, purely to escape the clutch of the customs authorities.

Nowadays, VRSA (as the Portuguese like to refer to the border town) is home to around 12,000 people. The bustling town centre with its grid layout is ideal for exploring on foot. Start on the Avenida da República, the grand avenue running along the seafront with its yacht harbour and weighty statue of the town's founder, the Marquês de Pombal. The *main square* with its star-shaped paving and adjoining church and town hall is named after him and forms the centre point of the town. From here, you will find your way with ease into all the busy shopping streets. The inviting stores and large selection of textiles and household items are very popular with Spaniards who stream in by ferry from neighbouring Ayamonte or via the motorway bridge.

EATING & DRINKING

A row of restaurants can be found in the extensive pedestrian precinct on the *Avenida da República*. They are all good and reasonably priced. The city's Spanish neighbours are aware of this and the spectacular waterfront is where they come to hang out.

ASSOCIAÇÃO NAVAL

Welcome to the yacht club – stylish atmosphere directly on the Rio Guadiana, serving fresh, top-quality seafood and with a large selection of tapas. *Av. da República | tel. 2 81 51 30 38 | www.anguadiana. com | €€*

SPORT & ACTIVITIES

INSIDER TIP
A walk in the woods

The wooded dunes are a dream for those wanting to exercise even in the heat of the summer. You can walk or even jog with a good sea breeze and a bit of shade to stop you overheating. The coast from Vila Real de Santo António to Monte Gordo is a small natural park, the *Mata Nacional das Dunas Litorais*, which is particularly important for the conservation of chameleons.

If you feel like swinging between the trees, the 🎭 *Parque Aventura (parqueaventura.net/vrsa)* offers a great fun space to explore the treetops. An ideal place to keep anyone with lots of energy entertained.

The moment you see the Rio Guadiana, you will find its allure hard to escape and a 🎭 boat trip is a must. Climb aboard to explore this highly fertile valley filled with groves of olives, oranges, figs and lemons on all sides. Between them, their lifeblood – the silvery tidal river – flows to *Mértola*. This river is also popular with sailors who love to anchor in it as there are no overnight fees. There are several companies offering boat tours (often including lunch). Two good options are *Trans Guadiana (transguadiana. com)* and *Rio Sul (riosultravel.com)*. Most companies will take you out to *Foz de Odeleite* and back.

BEACHES

The *Praia da Ponta da Areia* and *Praia de Santo António* just by the pier at the mouth of the river are still relatively untouched by human development. If you want beaches with the kind of infrastructure that comes with development, head to the resort of *Monte Gordo* (pop. 3,300), 4km to the west. With a host of concrete hotels, it is not going to win any prizes for beauty but if they were to give out prizes for lovely beaches with great views of fishing boats out at sea, it would be in with a good chance.

The 🌴 *Praia Verde* more than lives up to its name. Seven kilometres west of VRSA, this "green beach" is tucked away among dunes covered in vegetation. The erstwhile fishing village of *Manta Rota* 4km further to the west is more relaxed than Monte Gordo. In

Manta Rota's beach shimmering in evening light

general the beaches around VRSA are much less busy than the those on the rocky part of the Algarve coast. And if you have had enough of Portuguese beaches by this point … there are plenty to explore just across the border in Spain.

WELLNESS

The Algarve is not a region blessed with lots of hot springs like much of the Mediterranean. As a result, the fact you can take a salt bath at *Spa Salino* in the *Água Mãe (summer only: Tue–Sun 10am–7pm | Salina Barquinha, Castro Marim | FB: aguamae)* is even more of a luxury. *Água Mãe* does not only produce table salt, it also uses it for a huge variety of spa activities from yoga on a salt flat to salt-based facemasks.

NIGHTLIFE

In the summer, nearby *Monte Gordo* is the hub of the area's nightlife. The *casino* has a relaxed atmosphere. Bars and clubs are open until the early hours.

AROUND VILA REAL DE SANTO ANTÓNIO

🚺 CASTRO MARIM
4km north of Vila Real de Santo António / 5 mins by car on the N 122
In the 14th century this "fort on the coast" was the headquarters for the

Alcoutim: this statue of a Customs official keeps an eye on Spain across the river

powerful Order of Christ, which was headed by Prince Henry the Navigator from the beginning of the 15th century. The well-preserved ruins of the *castelo (daily 9am–5pm, summer 9am–7pm | admission 1.40 euros)*, 4km north of Vila Real de Santo António, are a reminder of a period of great splendour. The fortress protected the border to Spain well into the 17th century. These ruins serve as the backdrop to *Dias Medievais* or "medieval days", a fantastic historical festival that takes place at the end of August. The castle parapet gives you a full view of its counterpart *Forte de São Sebastião* on a hill nearby (closed to visitors) as well as the Rio Guadiana's expansive estuary and saltworks. *R5*

12 RESERVA NATURAL DO SAPAL DE CASTRO MARIM

Information centre 8km north of Vila Real de Santo António / 13 mins by car

One of Portugal's most important wetland areas lies in the estuary of the Rio Guadiana. Two-thirds of the approximately 21km² area is covered in water and it is a favoured breeding ground for many aquatic bird species, among them flamingos. Many migratory birds also come here in the winter. Birdwatching is possible near the *information centre* (close to the motorway bridge) and around the salt marshes. *R5–6*

🔢 ALCOUTIM ⭐

40km north of Vila Real de Santo António / 35 mins by car on the IC 27/N 122-1

The drive to Alcoutim via the Odeleite reservoir is by far and away the prettiest way to get there. Alcoutim is technically a small town but, with a population of around 1,000, it has a distinctly sleepy villagey feel. The 14th-century *castelo (daily 9am–5pm, summer 9am–7pm | admission 2.50 euros)* is charming rather imposing. Dating back to the 16th century, the *Igreja Matriz* is also an interesting sight, being one of the Algarve's first Renaissance churches.

Situated 8km further south, the *Museo do Rio (Tue–Sat 9am–1pm, 2–5pm (summer 10am–1pm, 2–6pm | admission 2.50 euros (combined ticket with other institutions in the region, e.g. the castelo) | Guerreiros do Rio)* provides an insight into the people living on the Rio Guadiana

and the central role of fishing and smuggling in this area.

Those after an adrenaline kick can zipline over the border from Spain (see p. 131). Freshwater swimming in a dammed river is possible at the attractive beach of *Praia Fluvial Pego Fundo* (signposted). Enjoy a meal afterwards on the village square in the restaurant *O Camané (tel. 9 64 10 85 85 | €–€€)*. About 6km to the south, you'll find a very traditional village restaurant called *Cantarinha do Guadiana (closed Wed | Montinho das Laranjeiras | tel. 2 81 54 71 96 | €€)*. They cook from the heart and it shows in their delicious, hearty and above all homely food.

Alcoutim is the starting point of *Via Algarviana*, a long-distance hiking trail which takes walkers for more than 300km through the hinterland to the *Cabo de São Vicente*. There are also plenty of other pretty footpaths and circular walks nearby. 📖 *R2*

WHERE TO SLEEP IN THE SOTAVENTO

A RUSTIC SPOT BETWEEN MOUNTAINS & SEA

There are few better spots to relax and get away from it all than the *Herdade da Corte (Sitio da Corte | tel. 2 81 97 16 25 | herdadedacorte.com | €€)* in the countryside around Tavira.

The main house here dates back to the 19th century and was once the centre of a large farm. Today's hotel is split between two buildings, the Monte do Lavrador and the Monte da Beleza, each of which sits atop a hill

in the Barrocal. It is hard to imagine a better spot to see the natural world in the Algarve. There are only 12 rooms, all of which are within easy reach of the unheated, saltwater swimming pool. A delicious, sedate breakfast is served on the hotel's tranquil terrace.

Tavira with its sights and restaurants is just 11km or a 15-minute drive away and, if you don't fancy the drive, you can always sign up for dinner in the Herdade.

THE BARLAVENTO

PICTURE-PERFECT ROCKY BAYS

The otherworldly cliffs on this rocky coastline glow in every shade of red and yellow and provide the perfect natural frame for a classic Algarve photo. The cliffs surround the idyllic sandy coves of the Western Algarve, known as the Barlavento, or "windward" coast, considered to be one of the most beautiful beach landscapes in Europe.

Over the millennia, the wind and the waves have sculpted the soft limestone cliffs into incredible shapes and stunning little coves,

Ponta da Piedade: the Algarve is famous for its striking rocky coastline

where visitors often have to descend narrow wooden steps in order to reach the clear, turquoise water. The landscape also opens up at certain points, with longer sandy beaches appearing at the mouths of rivers. Around these, some of the region's thriving tourist hubs have developed, with golf courses, shops and nightclubs to keep you occupied at all hours of the day. A paradise for those into beach life and nightlife, the Barlavento is also a great destination if you're looking for water sports or spectacular coastal walks.

THE BARLAVENTO

MARCO POLO HIGHLIGHTS

★ LAGOS
Harbour city with a golden chapel, a rich history and plenty of bars ➤ p. 68

★ PONTA DA PIEDADE
A lighthouse, ochre-coloured cliffs and amazing rock formations ➤ p. 72

★ ALBUFEIRA
Holiday atmosphere, lively night scene, great beaches ➤ p. 76

★ NOSSA SENHORA DA ROCHA
Could it be more photogenic? A white chapel perched high on the red-orange cliffs ➤ p. 82

★ **VILAMOURA**
Chic yachting hotspot for the rich and famous ➤ p. 84

★ **FERRAGUDO**
Picturesque fishing village at the mouth of the Rio Arade ➤ p.91

★ **ALVOR**
Old fishing town with a huge beach, a lagoon and an ornate church portal ➤ p. 90

Gomes Aires

Santana da Serra

Santa Clara-a-Nova

IC1

A2

IC1

A2

São Bartolomeu de Messines

Alte

Canhestris

Benafim

124

Silves

48km, 1 hr

A2

11 Paderne

Algoz

Tunes

IC1

A22

A22

Boliqueime

Lagoa

16

17 Fiesa

Alcantarilha **6**

9 Guia

Ferreiras

9.5km 3½ hrs

7 Armação de Pêra

Carvoeiro

10

8 Lagoa dos Salgados

Praia da Falésia

12

Praia da Marinha

Nossa Senhora da Rocha ★

Albufeira ★
p. 76

Vilamoura ★

4 km
2.49 mi

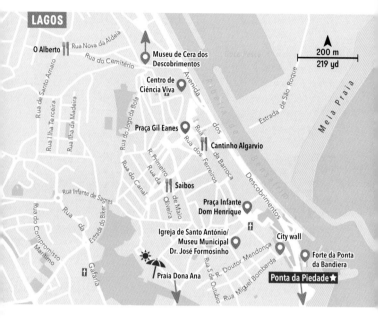

LAGOS

O Alberto
Rua Nova da Aldeia
Rua do Cemitério
Museu de Cera dos Descobrimentos
Centro de Ciência Viva
Rua de Santo Amaro
Rua Ilha Terceira
Rua Ilha da Madeira
Rua da Jogoda Bola
Avenida
Praça Gil Eanes
Rua dos Ferreiros
da Barroca
Cantinho Algarvio
R. Primeiro
Rua
do Canal
Rua
Infante de Sagres
Estrada do Biker
Rua
da
Rua do Compromisso
Marítimo
Galaria
de Maio
Oliveira
Saibos
Praça Infante Dom Henrique
Igreja de Santo António/ Museu Municipal Dr. José Formosinho
Rua 5 de Outubro
R. Doutor Mendonça
City wall
Praia Dona Ana
Rua Miguel Bombarda
Forte da Ponta da Bandeira
Ponta da Piedade ★

dos
Descobrimentos
Estrada de São Roque
Meia Praia
200 m
219 yd

LAGOS

(📖 E6–7) **Welcome to ★ Lagos! Whether you take a stroll through the lively streets of the old town, go for a swim on the long sandy beach or in the various small coves nearby, or take to the water to explore the unique grottos and rocky pinnacles of the Ponta da Piedade, you'll feel like you're in paradise! What's more, the former capital of the Algarve also has plenty of history and culture to offer.**

The mouth of the Ribeira de Bensafrim served as a sheltered mooring for the Phoenicians before the city of Lacobriga was founded here in the Roman period. Today, Lagos (pop. 23,000) is the most important town on the coast of the western Algarve; as you wander through the old town, which is still almost entirely encircled by a city wall, you will find many traces of its former significance, including statues that hark back to Portugal's Age of Discovery. At that time, Lagos was the last safe harbour that ships could call at before heading into the stormy Atlantic. Henry the Navigator sent forth his caravels from here onto the world's oceans in the 15th century, and at various points thereafter the majority of Portugal's trade with the rest of the world was conducted via Lagos. However, this is also where the decline of Portugal's Golden Age began. In 1578, the young King Sebastião had the misguided idea to fight Islam in Morocco. He set off from Lagos with 20,000 soldiers. Only a few returned, and the king was not among them. Portugal subsequently became a Spanish province for 60 years and, by the time it became independent once again, the English and Dutch had picked its colonial empire to pieces. With the earthquake in 1755, this once great city's downfall was complete – it only began to regain its identity with the advent of tourism in the 20th century.

SIGHTSEEING

FORTE DA PONTA DA BANDEIRA

The 17th-century builders of this fort certainly knew what they were doing. Tucked in at the point where the harbour's canal flows into the city, it could not have been better placed to protect the city from pirates. Ideal for defence then, today its location means that it has superb views of the rocky cliffs and soft sand combination that makes Lagos such an attractive place. A drawbridge leads into the well-preserved fortress, which contains a small, *azulejo*-lined chapel and hosts occasional exhibitions on a wide array of subjects. *Tue–Sun 10am–12.30pm and 2pm–5.30pm | admission 2 euros*

CITY WALL

You can gain a hugely varied perspective on Lagos by taking a walk along the astonishingly well-preserved city wall. Its current form dates back to the 16th century, but a defensive boundary was already in place during Roman and Moorish times. The most representative section can be found in the small *Jardim da Constituição* park between the Praça Infante Dom Henrique and the *Arco de São Gonçalo*, an attractive Moorish gate, which today bears the name of the town's patron saint. If you walk along the western section of the *muralha* you will scarcely find any tourists; here, the narrow streets of the old town grow increasingly quiet and very few of the buildings have been spruced up. Local residents walk their dogs in the patches of green and bits of wasteland behind the walls. It is worth getting to know this "other" side to Lagos – not least because local street artists express their creativity on some of the walls in this part of town.

The imposing Forte da Ponta da Bandeira was built to protect Lagos' harbour

PRAÇA INFANTE DOM HENRIQUE

Henrique, or Henry the Navigator sits proudly in the middle of Lagos' central square, surveying his surroundings and checking out the view all the way down to the Meia Praia. The sea view may seem apt, but it is likely it would have turned the famous navigator king green – he suffered badly from seasickness. Several historic buildings line the *praça*: in the direction of the sea lies the former *governor's palace* (seat of Algarve governors from the 14th century onwards). The small Manueline window at the far right is reputed to be where Sebastian made his final address to the people before setting out on his fatal expedition to North Africa – his failure to return meant the Portuguese throne was left empty ready for the Spanish to take over. On the right of the palace is the baroque *Igreja Santa Maria*. To the left of the large white customs house at the northern end of the square stands the former *slave market*. This is where the first official sale of African slaves took place in 1444, marking the beginning of the European slave trade at the start of colonial period. This dark chapter in the city's history is traced in the *Mercado de Escravos*, a small, interactive museum *(Tue–Sun 10am–12.30pm and 2–5.30pm | admission 3 euros | combined ticket with the city museum 5 euros)*. During construction of the underground car park to the north of the square, excavations revealed the human remains of a large number of people of African descent and evidence of the brutality of the slave trade. It seems likely that slaves who had died on the journey from Africa were simply thrown overboard on arrival. The same excavations also uncovered 3,000-year-old sandstone blocks that the Phoenicians had used to construct the town's first quay.

INSIDER TIP
Ancient harbour tucked away in a cellar

IGREJA DE SANTO ANTÓNIO/MUSEU MUNICIPAL DR. JOSÉ FORMOSINHO

The municipal museum of Lagos is referred to by some people as the "attic museum", as it apparently displays everything that has ever been unearthed in the attics of the town. Yet, even if the exhibits are something of a mish-mash, this doesn't quite do justice to the varied displays you can find here, and its recent renovations mean it is now a wonderful place to explore. There are artefacts from the Roman and Muslim eras, as well as coins, sacred art, paintings, traditional clothing, models of farms and fisheries, and much more besides. However, the undoubted highlight is the 18th-century Baroque *chapel of St Anthony*, which is only accessible via the museum. With its opulent *talha dourada* (gilded wood carving) and azulejos, its interior is one of the most magnificent on the Algarve. The paintings along the walls depict the miracles of St. Anthony of Padua, who was born in Lisbon in 1195 and is extremely popular in Portugal. *Tue–Sun 10am–12.30pm and 2–5.30pm | admission 3 euros | Rua General Alberto Carlos da Silveira*

Henry the Navigator lords it over the central Praça Infante Dom Henrique in Lagos

PRAÇA GIL EANES

This square causes confusion, and not because of the sheer number of cafés and shops in the alleyways round about that can be disorienting. The real problem arises from the square's name and the statue at its centre. The *praça* is named after the Lagos native Gil Eanes, who – under Henry the Navigator's influence – was the first person to sail round Cape Bojador in 1434. But the statue in the square depicts the far more tragic figure of King Sebastian. Erected in 1970 by the frequently misunderstood sculptor João Cutileiro, the statue seems almost child-like and makes the king look more like Saint-Exupery's *Little Prince* or even a young astronaut than an all-powerful ruler. The town's only memorial to Gil Eanes is a bronze statue in the *Jardim da Constituição*.

CENTRO DE CIÊNCIA VIVA

Engage their hands, their brains and their imagination! This interactive science museum, housed in a colourful pink building from the 17th century, teaches kids what the Portuguese journeys of discovery were all about. They can also find out how to communicate at sea and discover how a submarine works – plus much more besides! It's playful and fun for family members at all ends of the age spectrum. *Tue–Sun 10am–6pm | admission 5 euros, children (6–17) 2.50 euros | Rua Dr. Faria e Silva 34 (above the covered market) | lagos.cienciaviva.pt*

MUSEU DE CERA DOS DESCOBRIMENTOS

Do you want to find out more about the 15th and 16th centuries when the Portuguese became the first Europeans (at least since the Vikings) to discover lands across the sea? Hidden in a corner of the marina, this wax figure museum dedicated to the Portuguese age of discoveries ("Descobrimentos") may be small, but it is perfectly formed. It traces history through the experiences of a variety of important figures, including Prince Henry the Navigator, King Manuel I, Vasco da Gama and Magellan. *Daily 10am–5pm, until 7pm in summer | admission 6 euros, children (6–15) 4 euros | Marina da Lagos | Edificio Astrolábio | museuceradescobrimentos.com*

PONTA DA PIEDADE ★

The colourful magnificence of the Algarve coast in all its geological diversity … and all in one place. Exploring the wonderful landscape of "Piety Point" on foot should be on every Algarve itinerary. Narrow paths run along the edge of the red cliffs, which reach up to 40m high in places, while steep staircases take you down to stunning beaches such as *Praia Dona Ana* and *Praia do Camilo*. But the highlight of this narrow promontory is the lighthouse on its tip, which sits majestically above craggy cliffs that are characterised by grottoes, caves and towering rocks. If you follow the stairs down from the lighthouse, you will find a truly extraordinary jetty tucked into a cave. If the tide is right, there is nowhere better to start a boat trip along the coast.

EATING & DRINKING

CANTINHO ALGARVIO

It's often difficult to find a table in this pleasant and long-established restaurant in the pedestrian zone – and it's easy to understand why once you've

Glass-clear water, super-fine sand and golden cliffs at Praia Dona Ana

tasted the delicious seafood on offer here. *Closed Sun | Rua Afonso D'Almeida 17 | tel. 2 82 76 12 89 | ocantinhoalgarvio.pt | €€*

O ALBERTO

Guests here can see for themselves that everything is cooked from scratch. Watching Alberto at work in the kitchen is generally more entertaining than watching the TV shows that play in the background at this typical Portuguese restaurant. Delicious *cataplanas*, as well as fish and meat dishes, are brought to the table by Dona Odette herself. *Closed Sun | Largo Convento Senhora Glória 27 | tel. 2 82 76 93 87 | restauranteoalberto.pt | €€*

SAIBOS

Youthful, relaxed and a little different. Get away from the crowds here and sample creative variations on Portuguese classics, as well as delicious tapas (including vegetarian options). *Closed Sun in winter | Rua Marreiros Neto 45 | tel. 2 82 09 46 90 | FB: Saibos.restaurante | €–€€*

SHOPPING

The old town is chock-a-block full of shops. A lot of them (perhaps even the majority) sell mostly tourist tat, but there are great things to be found too. For particularly beautiful ceramics, head to *Galeria JJ Mealha (Rua Dr. José Cabrita 3 | FB: MealhaCeramics)*. The *indoor market hall (Av. dos Descobrimentos)* is well worth a visit, especially if you are after some fresh produce: fish is sold on the ground floor, and fruit and vegetables are on the first floor. From the roof terrace, there's a view of the marina.

SPORT & ACTIVITIES

Everywhere in Lagos you can buy tickets for 😮 boat trips to the grottos of the Ponta da Piedade. Whether you choose to relax aboard a sailing boat with *Bom Dia Boat Trips (bomdia-boattrips.com)*, or opt for the sporty option and hire a kayak (from e.g. *kayak-lagos.com*) or a stand-up paddleboard (from e.g. *kainuisup.com*) – exploring this rocky coast is a must! There's a lot to see under the water too, for example with Elmar and Ute's diving school *(blue-ocean-divers.eu)*. Enjoy mini golf? By the western gate of the city walls a minigolf course sits resplendent on the

INSIDER TIP
Rooftop minigolf

roof of a multi-storey car park. It is remarkably tastefully done with small ponds and modern art in between the holes *(proputtinggarden.com)*.

BEACHES

Stretching out to the east of Lagos is *Meia Praia* – a vast sandy beach that goes on for kilometres beyond the railway line (fortunately not a big distraction), curving all the way to the Ria de Alvor. Surfers, kite surfers and windsurfers alike love the swell that you get here. Directly alongside the harbour fort is where the beaches of the Ponta da Piedade begin, from *Praia Dona Ana* (a favourite because of its unique rocks) to *Praia do Camilo*.

To the west of the Ponta lies *Porto Mós*, a slightly larger bay surrounded by cliffs with a beautiful beach. The *Praia da Luz* is similarly wide and very popular in summer. The further west you go, the emptier and more secluded the beaches become.

NIGHTLIFE

The lanes north of the Praça Infante Dom Henrique and the roof of the multi-storey car park are the places to be in the evenings. The live music bar *Stevie-Ray's (Rua Senhora da Graça 9 | stevie-rays.com)* offers something for jazz and blues enthusiasts even in the off-season, starting late on Fri and Sat. For great cocktails, head to *Lendas Bar (Avenida dos Descobrimentos | FB: lendasbar)*. There are also fabulous drinks at the (almost) cosy *MJ's Bar (Travessa de Senhora da Graça 2 | FB:*

MJ's Bar Lagos); the cocktails are made by Marilyn, the owner, and she is also always happy to play whatever music you want.

AROUND LAGOS

🔟 BARRAGEM DA BRAVURA
15km north of Lagos / 20 mins by car on the N 125/N 125-9
A charming trail – especially in the spring when the meadows are in bloom – leads you via *Odiáxere* to this reservoir, constructed in 1958. It is surrounded by forested hills that are ideal for a picnic or for hiking. *D–E5*

🔟 ZOO DE LAGOS 😺
12 km northwest of Lagos / 17 mins by car on the N 125/M 532-1
Exotic animals, including birds and primates, are kept in species-appropriate surroundings in this charming and well-maintained private zoo. The kangaroos, for example, leap around a large enclosure with plenty of space, while peacocks strut around the paths and flamingos balance on one leg in the zoo's own small lake. The petting zoo allows smaller visitors an opportunity to meet animals up close and personally. *Sítio do Medronhal | Barão de São João | April–Sept daily 10am–7pm, Oct–March daily 10am–5pm | admission 18 euros, children 4-11 14 euros | zoolagos.com | D6*

3 LUZ

8km west of Lagos / 12 mins by car on the N 125

Sadly, the resort of Luz (pop. 3,500) is forever associated in many people's minds with the disappearance of Maddie McCann, the young girl that went missing here during a family holiday in 2007. If you can set the tragedy aside, then the town has plenty to offer visitors – a stunning beach, a small chapel, numerous welcoming restaurants and a charming promenade lined with lampposts and palm trees where excavations have revealed the remains of a Roman site. *D7*

4 BURGAU

13km west of Lagos / 20 mins by car on the N 125

This old, still very traditional fishing village is popular for its small beach and village pubs. The surroundings offer plenty of unspoilt nature, and you can hike along the cliffs to the ruins of the 17th-century *Forte de Almádena* close to the *Praia da Boca do Rio* (approx. 3km). Archaeological finds have proven that this small estuary was settled by the Romans. *D7*

5 SALEMA

20km west of Lagos / 25 mins by car on the N 125

This idyllic village, nestled in a little valley by the coast, is so pretty that even dinosaurs once enjoyed hanging out here – their footprints can still be seen in the rocks on the beach. The beach is flanked by huge, dramatic cliffs on both sides. A good spot from which to watch the sun go down while

There's a relaxed holiday atmosphere on the beach promenade at Luz

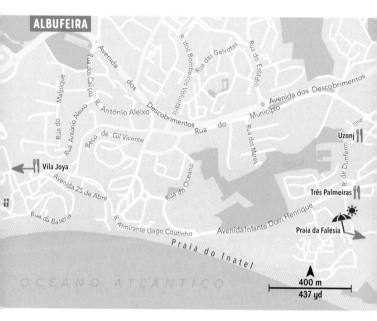

tucking into delicious Portuguese grub is *A Boia (Rua dos Pescadores 101 | tel. 2 82 69 53 82 | €€).* ⊞ *C7*

ALBUFEIRA

(⊞ J7) **At first glance, this former fishing village may appear to be an unappealing and built-up holiday resort – especially at the height of the summer when thousands of tourists descend on the town to take advantage of its vibrant nightlife. However, over time you may well come to love ★ Albufeira, thanks to the fantastic beaches both in the middle of town and in the immediate surrounding area.**

As a holiday destination, Albufeira (pop. 23,000) has a few unbeatable advantages over other towns. Its central location at the heart of the Algarve makes it a superb starting point for day trips in every direction; however, the large selection of cafés and shops in the city centre are also a genuine bonus for those who like to wander and browse or sit and relax in a lively resort. And then there's the legendary strip – a street full of bars and clubs that is a byword for vibrant nightlife on the Algarve. In other words, it is a great place to party – as long as you are not put off by the large number of stag and hen dos. Despite all the crowds, it is still possible to find a few quiet corners in Albufeira among the picturesque streets of the historic *Praia do Peneco* quarter high above the beach, or in the small *Parque de Vale Faro* above the *Praia do Inatel*.

SIGHTSEEING

In the historic heart of the city perched high above the beach, it is still possible to find a few faint traces of the era of Moorish rule, from which the name of the town ("Al-Buhera" – the lagoon) is derived. This hilltop location was once the site of a fortress that defended the settlement. The Rua da Bateria runs along the edge of a cliff and offers superb views over the beaches and the rocky coast, while the tiny *Misericórdia chapel* boasts a Gothic doorway that survived the 1755 earthquake. Housed inside the former town hall, the *Museu Municipal de Arqueologia (closed Mon | admission 1 euro | Praça da República 1)* displays artefacts from the Roman and Moorish eras.

Still up for some history? To the west of the main pedestrian street, Rua 5 de Outubro, you can visit three beautiful churches: the 18th-century *Igreja Matriz* parish church; the small *Igreja de São Sebastião*, which features a Manueline side door and is now used as a museum *(Museu de Arte Sacra | closed Mon | admission 2 euros)*, and the Baroque *Igreja de Sant'Ana*. The *Miradouro Pau da Bandeira* to the east of the *Praia dos Pescadores* offers great views over Albufeira, with an escalator taking you to the top.

EATING & DRINKING

TRÊS PALMEIRAS

It's no wonder that this pleasant restaurant has been open since 1987 and is still packed every evening. It

A musical performance in Albufeira's old town

was run by the same family for decades, and even though they've now handed the business on, their passion for good, traditional Algarve cuisine remains. The main focus of the menu is seafood – the *cataplanas* are delicious. *Closed Sun | Av. Infante Dom Henrique 51 | tel. 2 89 51 54 23 | restaurantetrespalmeiras.com | €€*

UZONJ

You might be left wondering how such a cool and fashionable venue can be so reasonably priced! You can eat a full meal at this grill restaurant for under 10 euros, and yet no expense is spared when it comes to culinary refinement or friendly staff. *Rua Dunfermline | mob. 9 17 84 76 21 | FB: uzonj restaurantegrill | €*

VILA JOYA

If you want to eat somewhere seriously refined and with incredible sea views, then treat yourself to an evening at this two-Michelin-starred gourmet restaurant run by Austrian Chef Dieter Koschina. You'll be boring your friends about the food for weeks, months, even years afterwards! *Closed Nov-Feb, otherwise open daily | Estrada da Galé | tel. 2 89 59 17 95 | vilajoya. com | €€€*

SHOPPING

The alleyways around the pedestrianised streets of Rua 5 de Outubro, Rua Cândido dos Reis and Largo Cais Herculano are full of shops offering all kinds of cheap tourist tat and

A kitsch-free souvenir: bags made from cork

knock-off clothes but buried among them are some great craft shops. Albufeiras's covered market (*Mercado Municipal dos Caliços | Largo do Mercado*) is on the way out of town to the east, just after the large Lidl store, and sells delicious fresh produce from local farmers and fishermen. There is also a flea market held here on the second and third Saturdays of the month. On the roads into Albufeira you will see lots of 🐷 locals selling produce from their gardens. You are unlikely to taste such juicy oranges and melons anywhere else – and certainly not at these low prices!

discount online | *near Guia, on the N 125 | zoomarine.com*) has a regular programme of falconry and dolphin displays, but there are also plenty of opportunities to jump in and cool off. Both little and large climbing nuts will have a great time at the 🐵 *Parque Aventura (opening times vary by month. Check online. | Estrada de Santa Eulália | parqueaventura.net)* high-rope course. There are lots of routes for the "curious" *(from 4 years old, 12 euros),* "adventurous" *(from 8, 14 euros)* and the "fearless" *(from 12, 17 euros)* to chart their own course through the treetops.

SPORT & ACTIVITIES

Lots of boat trips along the coast set off from the colourful marina to the west of Albufeira, including some 🐵 dolphin-watching tours, such as *Dolphins Driven (April–Oct | 35 euros, children 5-12 20 euros | dolphins.pt).* On the *Praia dos Pescadores* you can have a go on a banana boat (other shaped inflatables are available) and footvolley tournaments are also regularly held here. The *Praia da Galé* is great for windsurfing.

The waterslide park 🐵 *Aqualand (June 10am–5pm, July–Sept 10am–6pm | admission 27 euros, children 5-10 20 euros | on the N125 | aqualand.pt)* near Alcantarilha offers all the water-based fun you would wish for. The large zoo and theme park 🐵 *Zoomarine (March–Nov, opening times vary by month. Check online | admission 29 euros, children up to 10 20 euros, children under 1m free, 10%*

BEACHES

There is no shortage of great beaches in and around Albufeira. Most holidaymakers frequent the two city beaches *Praia dos Pescadores* (near the Cais Herculano) and *Praia do Peneco* (accessed through the beach tunnel of the Rua 5 de Outubro or the lift from the Rua Latino Coelho). East of the town, the long, beautiful 🏖 *Praia da Falésia* with its shimmering red cliffs (near Olhos de Água) stands out from the rest of the competition. In the evening as the sun descends, the rock here takes on such a wealth of colour that a camera is every bit as important as a bikini for a day at the beach. Olhos de Água has a unique coastal attraction of its own, which gives the town its name. At low tide, pools of freshwater appear between the algae-covered rocks on the left side of the bay. This

INSIDER TIP
Eye of water

rare natural phenomenon is caused by springs bubbling to the surface. According to centuries of fishermen's legends, the springs are a sign that a woman drowned here and continues to cry in perpetuity. Located west of the city are pretty little beach coves with friendly 🍹 beach bars, such as the Praias *de São Rafael*, *do Castelo* or *do Evaristo*. The *Praia da Galé* stretches on for several kilometres to Salgados and is easy to get to despite its stunning location at the foot of grand cliffs.

WELLNESS

Do you need a proper massage or a lengthy soak in a luxurious jacuzzi? Then treat yourself to a spa session at the *Hotel Epic Sana (Pinhal do Concelho | Praia da Falésia | Olhos de Água | algarve.epic.sanahotels.com)*. The hotel has one of the best spas on the Algarve, and you do not have to be a guest to book a treatment.

NIGHTLIFE

At night Albufeira city centre gets lively, especially in the vicinity of the *Largo Duarte Pacheco* and along the *Rua Cândido dos Reis*. The bar scene is international, but Brits predominate. Live music blares from countless (often Irish) pubs. The (Portuguese) *Bar Sal Rosa (Praça Miguel Bombarda 2 | FB: barSalRosa)* in the old town serves delicious cocktails accompanied by great sea views. The second nightlife hotspot, known as the "Strip", is actually the *Avenida Sá Carneiro* in the Areias de São João district near the

Praia da Oura. Here, bars stand side by side offering something for everyone; the party really gets started after midnight. New bars open on and behind the strip all the time – explore everything there is to discover to your heart's content all the way through to sunrise. And, if you want to dance the night away, visit the Algarve's oldest club (it's certainly older than most of its present customers): *Kiss (July–Sept | admission from 15 euros | Rua Vasco da Gama)* has been packing people in since 1981.

AROUND ALBUFEIRA

🔟 ALCANTARILHA
10km northwest of Albufeira / 20 mins by car on the M 526

This village (2,500 inhabitants) will be popular with fans of gruesome and spooky sights: the *Capela dos Ossos* next to the village church was built in the 16th century out of thousands of bones. The 1,500 skeletons needed to put the building together came from a discarded cemetery which the new settlement wanted to turn into agricultural land. Need something to help recover from the chapel? A little way outside the village you can get to know Dona Edite and her superb wines. She took over the winery *Quinta João Clara (daily 9am–6pm | Vale de Lousas | mobile tel. 9 67 01 24 44 | joaoclara.*

INSIDER TIP
Fine wine

Colourful fishing boats wait for their next catch on the beach at Armação de Pêra

com) after the death of her husband and manages it so successfully that she has won lots of awards for her red, white and rosé wines. If you register in advance, then she will be happy to provide an English-language tour of the *quinta* and offer a tasting. ⌑ *H6*

🔟 ARMAÇÃO DE PÊRA
13km west of Albufeira / 20 mins by car on the M 526

Although ugly hotels and apartment blocks have turned this village (pop. 4,900) into a concrete jungle, there are places where it has retained its charm as a former fishing village – at the eastern end of town, for example, where colourful fishing boats lie on the beach, or in the narrow lanes near the white *St Anthony's chapel* and the former *harbour fort*. The waterfront has a promenade and a 🏖 long, wide, sandy beach, which is especially popular with families. There are lots of bars and restaurants near the beach: you can find particularly good fresh fish for a reasonable price at *Zé Leiteiro (closed Mon | Rua das Portas do Mar | tel. 2 82 31 45 51 | €–€€).*

As you explore, cast a glance at the casino built in 1936 in a perfect location on the coast. It has been empty and unused since the Carnation Revolution and is crying out to have new life breathed into it. Until that time, a decent arts and crafts market is held in the former slot machine room, where you can pick up decent souvenirs. ⌑ *H7*

8 LAGOA DOS SALGADOS

8km west of Albufeira / 15 mins by car on the Estrada das Sesmarias

Drive through the VidaMar resort to reach the car park at Lagoa dos Salgados. From here, a beautiful footpath follows the banks of the lagoon, which stretches out behind the extensive dunes of the Praia dos Salgados. This lagoon landscape is both a home and a seasonal stop-over for lots of bird species and is the perfect spot for birdwatching. The flamingos put on a particularly good show! Paths run west from here all the way to the Praia Grande at Armação de Pêra; heading east, you can walk through the dunes and along the coast as far as Praia da Galé. *H7*

9 GUIA

7km northwest of Albufeira / 10 mins by car on the M 526-1

People from across the Algarve make pilgrimages to the outwardly fairly bland village of Guia (pop. 4,200). There are three reasons for this: the first is *Zoomarine* (see p. 79), a huge zoo and theme park that attracts hundreds of visitors every day. The second reason is culinary. Guia is a mecca for fans of the most famous grilled chicken in Portugal. Virtually everyone here sells *frango piri-piri*, the spicy barbecue chicken, but it is particularly tasty at *Ramires (daily, no reservations July/Aug | Rua 5 de Abril 14 | tel. 2 89 56 12 32 | restauranteramires.com | €)* which has been honing its craft since 1964. The third reason to come here is *Algarve Shopping (daily | N 125 | algarve shopping.pt)*, a massive shopping mall with cinemas, plus dozens of shops, supermarkets and fast-food restaurants. There is plenty here for tourists and residents alike. *J6*

10 NOSSA SENHORA DA ROCHA ★

16km west of Albufeira / 25 mins by car on the M 526/N 269-1

In Alporchinhos, on the western edge of Armação de Pêra, a striking pilgrim's chapel perches on the clifftop with sweeping views of the coastline. It was built by fishermen in the 16th century, but you could be forgiven for thinking they were trying to attract social media followers even then. The combination of sea, cliffs and white chapel is so perfect that, if you add a sunset, it can all seem a bit too kitschy! Pillars from the sixth or seventh

Paderne's almond trees blossom in the early spring

centuries are a Visigoth testimony to early Christianity in the Algarve.

Brought your swimming stuff? At the foot of the 30-m-high cliffs, there are invitingly beautiful beaches. And if you are the walking type, this stretch of coast, as far as *Carvoeiro*, is unrivalled for the variety of its caves and rock formations, secluded coves, grottoes and arches. One rare feature are the many holes in the cliffs created by water crashing against the roof of caves from below. *H7*

⑪ PADERNE

12km north of Albufeira / 20 mins by car on the N 395

Fancy a quick trip into Moorish history? It is virtually impossible to miss the 12th-century hill fort of *Castelo de Paderne*. Not only is it right by the motorway, but it also stands in a picturesque landscape next to the little Ribeira da Quarteira. The local authority here is currently undertaking some much-needed restoration work on the fort, which means you can only visit on the first and third Wednesday of every month *(10am–6pm | admission free)*. All that is left of the old village of Paderne is a patch of rubble near the castle, as it was destroyed during the earthquake in 1755; the inhabitants resettled around 5km to the north. Close to modern Paderne you can go on an oenological and gastronomic discovery tour at *Veneza (closed Tue all day and Wed lunchtime | tel. 2 89 36 71 29 | restauranteveneza. com | €€–€€€)*, a genuinely family-run gourmet restaurant. Its wine cellar is well-stacked, and it offers a hearty cuisine with many excellent meat dishes and delicious desserts made with almonds, figs and carob. | *⑿ K7*

🔢 VILAMOURA ★

18km east of Albufeira / 30 mins by car on the M 526

The twin villages of Vilamoura-Quarteira (pop. 21,500) make an unusual pair: the beachfront settlement of Quarteira (now disfigured by concrete tower blocks built in the 1970s) grew from an actual village and as such has a parish church and a lively *mercado municipal* with an attractive fish hall. Whereas Vilamoura was designed completely from scratch as a tailormade holiday resort for wealthy visitors … with its own casino, of course. What makes Vilamoura so interesting is how artificial it is – from the casino to the crazily expensive yachts in the harbour to the sports cars on every corner, there is nothing here to remind you of life before high-end tourism. The harbour is lined with elegant bars and restaurants, and is the place on the Algarve where you are most likely to run into a Portuguese celebrity. If the decadence of the present day gets too much, head to the west of the marina where you can step back in time by visiting the *Cerro da Vila (daily 9.30am–12.30pm and 2–6pm | admission 3 euros)*, a large archaeological site and museum based around a Roman villa from the third century, where (among other things) fish salting took place. *⑿ K7*

PORTIMÃO

(⑿ F6) **The Algarve's second "proper" city after Faro may not be huge, but it is full of interesting contrasts. Down by the sea, the glorious Praia da Rocha gleams in the sun – a tourist resort if ever there was one; on the Rio Arade you will find plenty of nautical traffic and a great museum; while the historic centre, which is largely untouched by tourists, offers a perfectly normal (and perhaps even slightly run-down) inner-city atmosphere.**

With its many bland modern buildings and motorways, *Portimão* (pop. 45,500) may at first seem rather unappealing, forgettable and bleak. However, look more closely and you'll find some more enticing areas, not only the beach of *Praia da Rocha*, but also, for example, pretty *Jardim Visconde Bivar*, a park in the attractive palm-lined *Zona Ribeirinha* along the river.

The Phoenicians knew the Arade estuary as a good place to moor their ships, and the Romans named the settlement Portus Magnus, or great harbour. Today, the marina is one of the biggest in Portugal, and anyone travelling to the Algarve by cruise ship will dock in Portimão. The small wharves and the fishing industry also continue to play a role, and even though there are now only two canneries left, the lively sardine festival that is celebrated in August is a sign of what is valued by the people who live here.

PORTIMÃO

Pedra Mourinha

Hortelã · Taberna da Maré · Dona Barca

Avenida São João de Deus

A Casa da Isabel · Teatro Municipal de Portimão

Rua Direita · O Mané

Ponte Velha

Estrada de Alvor

Avenida V7

Avenida Miguel Bombarda

Rua da Cruz Vermelha

Avenida São Lourenço da Barrosa (V6)

Avenida do Brasil

Avenida Dom Carlos I

Avenida Guanaré

Museu de Portimão

Rua Sidónio Pais

Avenida 25 de Abril

Rua Jaime Palhinha

Avenida Engenheiro Francisco Bivar

Estrada da Rocha

Arade

Praia de Alvor

Variante 8

Rua da Falésia

Avenida das Comunidades Lusiadas

Mojito Temple Bar

Praia da Rocha

Avenida Tomás Cabreira

Avenida Rio Arade

Nana's Bar

400 m
437 yd

SIGHTSEEING

MUSEU DE PORTIMÃO

Where industry and culture meet! This former former fish-canning factory has been converted into a municipal museum that has managed to retain the building's architectural interest while also creating a fantastic local museum. It is well worth a visit – and not just when it's raining. The old machinery and an impressive film from 1946 show you how the cannery used to operate, and how the female workforce packed the sardines into tins. You will also learn all kinds of exciting facts about fishing and agriculture in this region, as well as about its prehistoric inhabitants. In addition, there is a changing programme of exhibitions on the top floor and in the old cistern in the cellar. *Tue 2.30–6pm (Aug 7.30–11pm) Wed–Sun 10am–6pm (Aug 3–11pm) | admission 3 euros,* ⚑ *free on Sun pm | Rua Dom Carlos | museudeportimao.pt*

PRAIA DA ROCHA ⚑

When people talk about the "beach of the rock", they don't just mean the marvellous long and wide sandy beach that separates Portimão from the Atlantic; rather, they are referring to an entire district of the city that developed at the beginning of the 20th century as a fashionable spa resort, complete with Art Deco villas and the first casino on the Algarve. Unfortunately, it has been rather defaced with a good deal of concrete over the decades; nonetheless, you can still wander along the beach for several kilometres and take advantage of countless cafés and bars. During the summer the whole place is packed. At the eastern end, near the mouth of the Rio Arade, the 17th-century harbour fortress, the *Fortaleza de Santa Catarina*, offers splendid views over the modern marina and across the river to Ferragudo. At the western end of the beach, the *Miradouro dos Três Castelos* sits on a promontory and provides glorious views of the *praias*.

PEDRA MOURINHA
If you feel the need to see something seriously strange, make a trip out to the industrial zone, *Pedra Mourinha*: on Rua de Pedra 5 there is a large boulder jutting out of the pavement. Geologists

INSIDER TIP
Stray rock

believe that the rock originally came from the Serra de Monchique, so how on earth did it end up here? Nobody knows! In the absence of a more scientific answer, generations of theories have led to a popular local explanation – a Moorish princess fell in love with a peasant boy in this area. When her father, the king, heard about the

relationship, he immediately packed the boy off to war where he promptly died near Monchique. The princess went to the site and her tears flowed all the way down from the mountains to Portimão where they formed into a rock … not a happy ending.

EATING & DRINKING

A CASA DA ISABEL
A visit to this tiny café rich in tradition is always worthwhile –if only for the decorative azulejo façade. But then you'll spot the vast quantities of homemade delicacies … a dream! Make sure you try Isabel's Trilogia Algarvia - a wonderfully sweet treat made from carob, almonds and figs. *Rua Direita 61 | tel. 2 82 48 43 15 | acasadaisabel.com | €*

INSIDER TIP
A dessert in three acts

Why were sardines canned? The Museu de Portimão provides the answer

DONA BARCA

They turn up the heat in this restaurant located under the old Arade bridge in order to serve up freshly grilled fish daily. In our opinion, this is the best place to get smoky grilled sardines in the summer. *Largo da Barca* | *tel. 2 82 48 41 89* | *FB: Dona Barca* | *€€*

HORTELÃ

Perhaps by this point in your holiday, you will have had enough of fish and will be in urgent need of something vegetarian. This relatively new arty and organic café/restaurant will satisfy all your cravings. There is a changing menu of well-presented and very fresh veggie dishes, as well as excellent snacks and desserts. Hortelã's fruit juices are also

INSIDER TIP
Smoothies with city views

superb and you can take them up to the roof, where a terrace offers great views across the town. *Closed Sun* | *Rua da Hortinha 10* | *tel. 9 30 55 17 80* | *FB: cafetaria.hortela* | *€*

O MANÉ

This untouristy place serving meat and seafood dishes is extremely popular with the locals. Give the delicious *Massada de Peixe* a try, a stew made up of fish and pasta, or go for the excellent *Carne de Porco à Alentejano*, a pork dish served with mussels. *Closed Sun* | *Largo Doutor Bastos 1* | *tel. 2 82 42 34 96* | | *FB: Restaurante O Mane* | *€-€€*

TABERNA DA MARÉ

While you wait for your food at this traditional tavern, you can admire a collection of old photos that show you what Portimão used to look like in days gone by. One of the best things on the menu is the grilled squid. *Closed Mon | Travessa da Barca 9 | tel. 2 82 41 46 14 | FB: tabernadamare |* €-€€

SHOPPING

Countless shops can be found in the pedestrianised streets of Rua do Comércio and Rua João de Deus, and while you explore, you'll also be getting to know Portimão's historical centre. The city's *covered market (Mon-Fri 7am–2pm and 5–7pm, Sat 7am–2pm | Avenida São João de Deus)* is the most modern in the Algarve with plenty of fresh local produce. At the *Parque de Feiras e Exposições* beyond the railway tracks there's a regional market on the first Monday of the month and a flea market on the first and third Sunday of the month.

The ☂ *Aqua Portimão* is a massive shopping centre with more than 130 shops, cinemas, restaurants, a large supermarket and everything that you need. It is on the main road into Portimão, so it is hard to miss.

SPORT & ACTIVITIES

All aboard! You can take some wonderful boat trips from Portimão, exploring the caves along the cliffs or up the river to Silves; the pleasure boat moorings are located on the waterfront by the beautiful *Jardim*

Climb aboard the *Santa Bernarda* for a tour of the coast

Visconde Bivar park. For an extra-special experience, try taking a trip on the two-masted cutter 🎭 *Santa Bernarda (tickets 35 euros, children (3–10) 20 euros | departures 9.45am and 2.20pm | tel. 2 82 42 27 91 | santabernarda.com)*, which has been converted into a caravel worthy of any pirate and is moored on the *Cais Vasco da Gama*.

Visitors with a PADI diving certificate and those who want to learn how to dive will find a highly professional diving centre at ⚓ *Subnauta (Rua Eng. José Bívar | Praia da Rocha | mobile tel. 9 35 57 70 00 | www.subnauta.pt)*. The team will take good care of you and guide you to the spectacular shipwrecks off the coast of Portimão.

If you would like to see the underwater world but are not keen on breathing from a tank, then a snorkelling trip is just the thing. Inês and Pedro from *Zip & Trip (Tel. 9 29 25 93 48 | zipandtripalgarve.com)* offer particularly interesting trips to sea caves and are happy to take your preferences into account.

If you are more into soaring in the sky than diving to the depths, the airport in Montes de Alvor may well offer you a perfect day out. The airfield is mainly used by a sky-diving company, *Skydive Algarve (tel. 9 14 26 68 32 | skydivealgarve.com)*, who will help you tick one unforgettable experience off your bucket list. In tandem with an experienced skydiver, you will leap from a plane into the air at 4000m.

INSIDER TIP
It's raining people

Children (and more than a few adults) will be in heaven at the the waterpark 🎭 *Slide & Splash (April–Oct, opening hours vary from month to month so check online | admission 27 euros, children (5–10) 20 euros | Lagoa | slidesplash.com | ⏱ plan a whole day!)*. The huge slides are designed for you to go fast so we strongly advise women to wear a well-fitting bikini or a full costume.

INSIDER TIP
Slide safely

BEACHES

No doubt about it: the ⚑ *Praia da Rocha* beach is the best advert for Portimão, thanks to its fine, soft sand and the long wooden promenade that passes many beach bars. There's lots going on here in summer, including beach volleyball and all sorts of water sports.

To the west are smaller bays with magnificent beaches protected by rocks: *Praia dos Três Castelos*, *Praia do Vau* or *Praia do Alemão*. There are also sections of coast here which are very difficult to access, such as *Praia do Caniço* near the Prainha resort with it's a *Restaurant-Bar Caniço (March–Oct | tel. 2 82 45 85 03 | www.canico restaurante.com | €€)* nestled between the rocks on the beach. The coastal landscape opens up again just at the point where the 🌴 *Praia de Alvor* begins. This huge beach is backed by dunes, which separate it from a lagoon that is home to a large number of interesting birds. Walk along the dunes for beautiful views of the Ria de Alvor.

MOJITO TEMPLE BAR

As the name suggests, you can find some superb mojitos here – as well as some wild dancing to trendy kizomba or salsa music. *Daily 10pm–4am | Rua António Feu | Praia da Rocha | FB: mojitotemplebar*

NANA'S BAR

This is where Portimão's young people meet for a beer or a gin and tonic. The atmosphere is relaxed, though there are occasional fancy-dress parties . *Daily noon–4pm | Rua José Bivar | Praia da Rocha| FB: Nanas Bar*

TEATRO MUNICIPAL DE PORTIMÃO

TEMPO located in the former city palace Sárrea is host to all kinds of cultural events: theatre, ballet, chanson, fado, puppet theatre, classical concerts and much more. Live music is also performed in its *Café Concerto. Largo 1° Dezembro | tel. 2 82 40 24 75 | teatromunicipaldeportimao.pt*

AROUND PORTIMÃO

🔟 ALVOR ⭐

7km west of Portimão / 10 mins by car on the M 531

The *Ria de Alvor* is a wonderfully quiet tidal lagoon in an environmentally protected area and serves as a relaxing retreat for people from across the region. Although a number of hotel complexes have sprung up at the edge of the fishing village of Alvor (pop. 6,100), it has retained an appealing atmosphere which is best experienced on a stroll through the village.

Make sure you visit the beautiful village church – the 16th-century *Igreja Matriz* – where you can marvel at the delicate stone carvings from the Manueline era. You'll find plenty of restaurants and bars in the old town, as well as in the harmonious *Zona Ribeirinha* with its broad promenade, including the basic *Taberna Zé Morgadinho (€-€€)* which exudes all the charm of a fishermen's pub. As it happens, the real fishermen aren't far away, and you can watch them go about their work at the port – which is also the starting point for various boat tours through the lagoon and out to sea. The *Praia de Alvor* is one of the best beaches in the area. *Ⅲ F6*

14 FERRAGUDO ★

*5km southeast of Portimão / 10 mins
by car on the Ponte Velha*

The white houses in this small fishing village (pop. 1,900) are spread out over a hill on the banks of the Arade and serve as a scenic counterpoint to the tower blocks across the water on the Praia da Rocha. Ferragudo has managed to preserve its picturesque charm despite everything that has happened around it. The main square of Praça Rainha Dona Leonor, located at sea level on the Rua 25 de Abril and on the *"Cais" (Rua Infante Santo)*, offers a range of pleasant cafés, grill restaurants and bars with live music. Make sure you also climb up through the maze of narrow streets and staircases to the *church*, as from here you can take in a wonderful view over Portimão and the river.

If you want to go for a swim then head for the beautiful beaches of *Praia da Angrinha* and *Praia Grande*, which are separated from each other by the (privately owned) harbour fortress *São João*. From the *Praia do Molhe* you can walk out onto the estuary breakwater, which extends a long way out into the sea. The beautiful *Farol da Ponta do Altar* lighthouse, which dates back to 1893, also offers superb views. The *Caminho dos Promontórios* allows you to walk along the rocky coast on a well-maintained path. If you go the full distance of 7km you will end up in Carvoeiro. ⊞ *F6*

15 CARVOEIRO

*11km east of Portimão / 20 mins
by car*

As recently as the late 20th century, fishermen set the tone at "charcoal burners' beach" but for a long time now, tourism has been the main source of income. The population of 2,800 expands to many times that number during the summer, leaving this attractive village with its many

One of the Algarve's most picturesque resorts: Ferragudo

Natural sculptures at Algar Seco

bars and cafés and the expansive holiday resorts surrounding it firmly in the hands of holidaymakers – the bulk of whom come from Germany. But you need only take a look at the region's sleepy coves with their sandy beaches – especially the glorious Praia da Marinha – to understand why it's such a popular spot. You can explore the unique coastal landscape and many of the (often deserted) coves on foot via the beautiful paths that run along the cliffs, in particular towards Armação de Pêra. Don't miss a stroll along the wooden boardwalk from Carvoeiro town centre to Algar Seco

INSIDER TIP
A wooden path to a rocky landscape

with its bizarre rock formations, caves and towers. It is just 1km away. Stop off at the pleasant *Boneca Bar (March–Oct | tel. 2 82 35 83 91 | €–€€)* to enjoy a drink with the bright red rocks as a fantastic backdrop. In the centre of Carvoeiro, *Ele & Ela (closed for lunch and all day on Mon | Rua do Barranco 28 | tel. 2 82 35 75 09 | €€)* delights its guests with unusual creations including lots of veggie options. *G7*

16 LAGOA

10km east of Portimão / 15 mins by car on the N 125

Most people who pass through Lagoa, do so while stuck in a traffic jam on the N125 and never realise what little treasures this administrative centre (pop. 7,200) has to offer. You can leave your car in the large car park in front of the Adega Cooperativa do Algarve wine cooperative. Be sure to sample some of their wines in the café by the entrance to the excellent private art gallery *Galeria de Arte* (Mon–Sat 10am–6pm | galeria-de-arte. net) housed in the same building.

INSIDER TIP
The art of wine

Next, take a stroll through the streets of the village's beautiful historic centre which are marked out by red tarmac. Refreshingly untouched by tourists, the historic centre has been amazingly well preserved. Most of the buildings date back to the 18th century, such as the baroque *Igreja Matriz* or the *Convento de São José* (now used as a cultural centre). The small *market hall* at the eastern end of the old town is also worth a look. If a trip there awakens your hunger, pay a visit to *Tapas no Bucho (usually closed Dec–March and on Sun | Rua Teofilo de Braga 1 | tel. 2 82 03 75 06 | FB: tapas nobucho | €)*. This is a family business which sources local ingredients for its delicious dishes. The huge advantage of the small portions is that you can give everything a go! *⎐ G6*

⓱ FIESA 😍

12km east of Portimão / 16 mins by car on the N 125

Building sandcastles is not just for kids. Every year artists from around the world come to this site near Lagoa to craft the most unbelievable constructions and landscapes from sand at the world's biggest sand sculpture festival. From June to September, the figures are illuminated at night, which creates a wonderful atmosphere. *March–Nov | admission 9.90 euros | children (6–12) 4.90 euros, 15% discount if you buy online | fiesa.org | ⎐ G6*

INSIDER TIP
Night in the sand museum

WHERE TO SLEEP IN THE BARLAVENTO

MINIMALIST, VINTAGE OR BOHO CHIC?

The hotel Casa Mãe (30 Zi. | Rua do Jogo da Bua 41 | Lagos | tel. 2 82 78 00 80 | casa-mae.com | €€) is located in the grounds of an old manor house directly abutting the western edge of the city walls. Despite its historical surroundings, it attracts a trendy, youthful clientele. Accommodation is arranged across three buildings which are described respectively as "minimalist", "vintage" and "boho chic". There is yoga on the roof terrace before breakfast (if the sun is shining), and the restaurant offers delicious Algarve food and runs cooking classes where you learn how to turn produce from the hotel's own garden into stunning dishes. And if you need a couple of presents to take home with you, spend some time browsing in the hotel's boutique. It sells top-quality clothes, cosmetics and accessories, all made in Portugal.

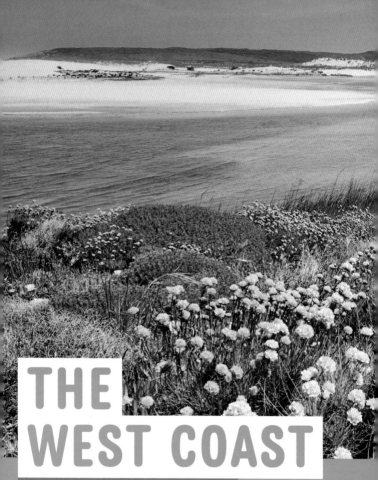

THE
WEST COAST

WIND, WAVES & WILDERNESS

In the Algarve's wild west you will find untouched landscapes such as the romantic and picturesque Costa Vicentina – a unique, isolated and sometimes rather hostile rocky coast where the wind whips through your hair and the waves are more suited to surfing than swimming.

The entire length of the Costa Vicentina is a protected nature reserve, and a wonderful long-distance trail runs all along this spectacular coast. The cliffs are interrupted here and there by valleys

Walkers and surfers are drawn to the natural beauty of the Costa Vicentina

where rivers have worn clefts in the rock; the resulting estuary lagoons open out onto wonderfully scenic beaches that are seldom crowded. The area is a little too raw for mass tourism; it appeals more to independent travellers clad in windcheaters.

It's well worth experiencing the magic of Europe's wild and romantic southwestern corner, even if only on a day trip – but if you have the time and the inclination, then this amazing landscape is ripe for exploring on foot.

THE WEST COAST

MARCO POLO HIGHLIGHTS

★ **SAGRES**
This harbour town has a fortress and sheltered beaches ➤ p. 98

★ **CABO DE SÃO VICENTE**
Europe's most southwesterly point is swept by wind and waves ➤ p. 101

★ **ARRIFANA**
There's a spectacular view of the crescent-shaped bay and the steep rocky coast ➤ p. 106

Praia de Odeceixe

Odeceixe **5**

120

Rogil

Praia Amoreira

Aljezur
p. 102

6 Arrifana ★

120

65 km, 1 hr 10 mins

Bordeira

7 Carrapateira

Praia do Amado

3 Pedralva

Barão de São Jo

Barão de São Miguel

268

Budens

Vila do Bispo **2**

4

Nossa Senhora de Guadalupe

Praia do Beliche

Cabo de São Vicente ★ **1**

● **Sagres ★**
p. 98

SAGRES

(□□ B8) **In days gone by, this place was thought to be the end of the world – so it's little wonder that the southwesternmost point of continental Europe projects an air of mystery and adventure.**

★ *Sagres* is still associated with 15th-century Portugal's spirit of discovery. However, even before then it served as a place of worship for the Moors and the Romans, and it was the latter who gave the area its name: *Promontorium Sacrum*, or "sacred headland". Today, Sagres is not just the name of the country's most southwesterly point but also the name of a well-known brand of Portuguese beer (although the beer is brewed in Lisbon).

Sagres (pop. 1,900) has changed a lot in recent years thanks to its most important resource: the seemingly endless stream of perfect surf that hits its shores. This has led to an explosion of hostels, surf camps and chilled-out cafés in this otherwise bland town. It is hard to point out a proper town centre, but the busiest spots are around the Praça da República and along the Rua Comandante Matoso – and of course, the stunningly beautiful beaches that all face in different directions, so that at least one of them will be sheltered from the wind on any given day.

SIGHTSEEING

FORTALEZA DE SAGRES
This rather over-zealously restored 17th-century fortress bars the way to the *Ponta de Sagres*, a barren rocky plateau that extends for a considerable distance into the turbulent sea. This is where Henry the Navigator stood in the 15th century and dreamed of striking out for new lands across the ocean – he may also have gathered scholars here to discuss and develop his plans. His dreams of discovery became reality thanks, in part, to new navigational techniques and the use of the more manoeuvrable caravel ship design. Within two generations, an insignificant region on the edge of Europe had become a wealthy seafaring nation.

The role played by Sagres's famous *rosa dos ventos* ("rose of the winds") in these developments will likely never be known. Discovered here in 1928, it consists of a paved circle, 43m across, marked out into segments that suggest it may have been used as a giant compass or a sundial. It is the first thing you see when you enter through the impregnable walls of the fortress. The only other original building is the small *Nossa Senhora da Graça* chapel, everything else here being a more modern addition. Ignore these recent eyesores and go for a stroll around the spit of land they are built on, as the real highlight here is the view from the top of the 60-m-high cliffs. *Daily 9.30am–5.30pm, until 8pm in summer | admission 3 euros*

PORTO DA BALEEIRA ⚑
It's worth making a detour down to the fishing port nestled at the eastern end of Sagres, where a few Algarvios still make their living from the fishing

Hang out in Sagres' enticing street cafés in the summertime

industry. Time your visit to coincide with the return of the colourful boats into the harbour, fully laden with fish. The action every afternoon at the *auction hall (Mon–Fri 7.30–10am and 3.30–8pm)* is very entertaining. Traders and chefs come from far and wide to bid on the valuable seafood, as the fish auction in Sagres is reputed to be one of the best in Europe.

EATING & DRINKING

A SEREIA
You won't find fresher fish anywhere else. Located above the auction room in Sagres's port, you will likely be surrounded by real fishermen as you tuck in to your lunch. *Mon–Fri 8am–7pm |* *Porto de Pesca da Baleeira | tel. 2 82 10 96 82 | FB: asereiasagres | €–€€*

ESTRELA DO MAR
This basic, down-to-earth place is a popular meeting spot for locals as well as tourists. It serves fish specialities, wine and beer. *Rua Comandante Matoso | tel. 2 82 62 40 65 | €*

NORTADA
Windsurfers are not the only people to frequent this popular restaurant on Martinhal beach. It serves great seafood, and the views of the sunset from here mark it out from the competition. *mobile tel. 9 18 61 34 10 | €€*

Surfers at Praia do Tonel wait for the perfect wave

VILA VELHA

This top-quality restaurant is elegant and relaxed. The high standard of its cuisine has made it one of the most popular places to eat in Sagres. Excellent wines accompany the dishes. *Dinner only, closed Mon | Rua António Patrão Faustino | tel. 2 82 62 47 88 | vilavelha-sagres.com | €€–€€€*

SPORT & ACTIVITIES

There are a number of surfing schools on this wave-riding riviera, including the *Freeride Surf Camp (frsurf.com)*. The sea around Sagres not only has the best waves in Portugal, it also has some of the richest fish stocks, making the region a paradise for scuba divers – contact the *Divers Cape diving school (www.diverscape.com)*. Speaking of wildlife: you can go on dolphin-watching tours with Marilimitado *(marilimitado.com)* or time your visit to attend the *birdwatching festival (birdwatchingsagres.com)* during the peak migration season at the start of October.

There are also two great long-distance trails for hikers, the *Via Algarviana (viaalgarviana.org)* and the *Rota Vicentina (rotavicentina.com)* both of which end at Cabo de São Vicente. The 10-km section of the Rota Vicentina that runs from the cape to the *Torre de Aspa* – the highest point on this coast at 156m – is breathtakingly beautiful yet surprisingly neglected by tourists.

BEACHES

While the *Praia da Mareta* beach, located in the middle of Sagres, is largely sheltered from the westerly winds, big waves that are perfect for surfing roll into shore to the west of the *ponta* at *Praia do Tonel* and *Praia do Beliche*. The latter is tucked under high cliffs and only accessible down a long wooden stairway. The *Praia do Martinhal* behind the fishing port is popular with windsurfers, and the offshore islands here are a sanctuary for birdlife and form an attractive backdrop. Around 15km east of Sagres lie the stunning rocky coves *Praia do Zavial* and *Praia da Ingrina*, which can be reached by car via Raposeira.

AROUND SAGRES

1 CABO DE SÃO VICENTE ★
6km west of Sagres / 8 mins by car on the N 268

An enormous lighthouse marks the most southwesterly point in continental Europe, where 70-m cliffs hold back the wind and waves. The cape is the most-visited destination on the Algarve, but the crowds tend to gather at the food and souvenir stands in the car park during the day. If you walk a short way along the cliffs to the north or east (taking extreme care, especially when it's windy!) or arrive at sunset, you can enjoy the magnificent scenery in peace.

The *lighthouse complex (daily June–Oct, closed Mon Nov–May)* was built in 1846, and its inner courtyard contains toilets, a shop, a café and a small *museum (admission 1.50 euros)* on the maritime history of the cape. The *lighthouse* itself is also open to the public *(Wed 2–5pm, admission free)*: the keeper simply opens the door from time to time and guides any waiting visitors through the facility. It is genuinely impressive, with 3,000-watt lamps that are visible from 90km away, making them among the most powerful in Europe.

A *hot dog stand (March–Oct daily 10.30am–5.30pm)* here has become famous far beyond the western Algarve because it sells genuine bratwurst imported directly from Germany, freshly grilled on the spot and served with a certificate confirming that you have just consumed the last bratwurst available on this side of the Atlantic. *B7*

2 VILA DO BISPO
10km (6 miles) north of Sagres / 10 mins by car on the N 268

The main landmark in this inland resort (pop. 950) is the old *water tower* perched at the town's highest point. The focal points of community life are the market building and the cafés lining the church square; beyond that the place is rather sleepy. However, the nearby beaches *Praia do Castelejo* and *Praia da Cordoama* are glorious and rarely crowded, even in summer.

Perhaps even more beautiful, though, is the hiking trail that leads all the way to the Cabo de São Vicente, 13km from Vila do Bispo along the clifftops – simply spectacular! *B–C7*

Whitewashed houses cluster below the castle ruins in Aljezur

🖪 PEDRALVA

20km north of Sagres / 20 mins by car on the N 268

This once almost-abandoned village has experienced a renaissance thanks to tourism, and its small houses have been renovated and can now be rented as traditional-style holiday homes. Even if you're not staying here, it's worth poking around the pictur-esque alleyways, especially as you might find yourself at *Pizza Pazza (evening only, closed Mon | tel. 2 82 63 91 73 | pizza-pazza-pedralva. business.site | €–€€)* which serves the best pizzas for miles around (book in advance!) | ⌘ C6

🖪 NOSSA SENHORA DE GUADALUPE

14km east of Sagres / 15 mins by car on the N 268/N

On the N 125 just after Raposeira, you will come across this unassuming white chapel – which is a rarity, as it is

believed to have been built shortly after the expulsion of the Moors in the 13th century, making it one of the old-est churches on the Algarve. It boasts many beautiful Romanesque and Gothic elements, from the small rose window to its keystones and capitals. *Closed Mon* | ⌘ C7

ALJEZUR

(⌘ D4) **It's easy to fall in love with Aljezur, which – with a population of 3,400 – is the biggest place in a very sparsely populated area. The village-sized town is so homely and welcoming that you'll want to start exploring straight away – starting in its steep, picturesque streets lined with whitewashed houses and then heading on to the ruins of its Moorish castle and the small, enchanting market hall by the river.**

It won't take you long to work out why so many people from other countries have moved to the area, especially when you realise how close it is to some stunning coves and beaches.

SIGHTSEEING

MUSEUMS

You will come across several museums as you walk up to the castle through the old town. The small *Museu de Arte Sacra (Rua São João de Deus)* next to the 16th-century *Igreja da Misericórdia* has a collection of religious exhibits, while the *Museu Municipal (Largo 5 de Outubro)* is housed in the 19th-century former town hall. One interesting room here is devoted to relics from the era of Muslim rule in the Middle Ages, while another contains an archaeological exhibition. Upstairs is an anthropological exhibition. For just 2.20 euros you can visit every museum

in town – including the *Museu Antoniano* inside the former chapel of St Anthony with its collection of contemporary church art, and the *Casa-Museu Pintor José Cercas*, formerly the home of the artist of the same name. *Tue–Sat 9am–1pm and 2–5pm (until 6pm in summer)*

CASTELO 🐷

Perched at the top of the hill, with stunning views down to the Ribeira de Aljezur, is the ruin of a Moorish castle which is free to visit. It has never been extensively restored and as a result blends even more imperceptibly into the landscape. It is a short ten-minute climb to get there (a little strenuous in the summer), but it's well worth every step for the stunning panoramic view over the green hills stretching to the Serra de Monchique on one side and the sea on the other. Information panels tell the story of this castle from the tenth century and how the Christian crusaders conquered it in the 13th century. You can also drive up by car, but the way through the village is more enjoyable.

EATING & DRINKING

BISTROT GULLI

If you fancy dining on some quirky Mediterranean creations then make your way to this bistro. The food is really something special – a feast for the eyes and the tastebuds alike. *Closed Mon | Sitio da Fonte de Santa Susana, 4km miles south on the EN 120 | tel. 2 82 99 43 44 | FB:gullibistrot | €€*

CAFÉ DO MERCADO

Friendly café next to the indoor market hall serving good-value snacks, perfect for a break from browsing the fresh produce next door. *Largo do Mercado* | €

MOAGEM

A huge group of people banded together to lovingly convert this old cornmill into an alternative cultural centre (offering yoga, exhibitions, concerts and much else) and a vegetarian restaurant. The restaurant, Mo Bistro, serves veggie takes on classic Portuguese dishes, all made with local produce. *Closed Sun | Rua João Dias Mendes 13–14 | tel. 9 25 28 90 81 | FB: moagemaljezur* | €

PONT'A PÉ

This cosy restaurant, café and bar is a stone's throw from the river and has become an institution thanks to its good hearty food. The best seats are on the terrace. Late in the evening, things really get going here – especially on balmy summer nights when people love to dance and party. *Closed Sun | Largo de Liberdade 12 | tel. 2 82 99 81 04 | pontape.pt* | €€

INSIDER TIP
Party at the ponte

SPORT & ACTIVITIES

🐾 Donkey trekking is not just a great holiday experience for kids. German expat Sofia von Mentzingen combines a donkey sanctuary (*Burros & Artes | tel 2 82 99 50 68 | esel wandern-algarve.blogspot.pt*) with a donkey-trekking business. The treks take in the Aljezur countryside and coast and last for 1½ hrs, half a day, a full day or even several days (*dates and prices on request*). It's sometimes unclear who is leading whom, but the good-tempered animals are carrying your bags, so perhaps they have the right to choose which way to go. The treks are so enjoyable that they sometimes lead to lifelong friendships developing between those who have taken part.

BEACHES

There are a lot of gorgeous bays near Aljezur. The sea can get pretty rough around here, which means surfers tend to like this stretch of coast more than swimmers. That said, the scenery is so stunning that a day at the beach here has its own charm – you will find it hard to track down a more romantic experience in the Algarve than watching the sun going down over the cliffs above a pretty cove.

The best local *praias* include Amado, Carrapateira, Arrifana, Monte Clérigo and Odeceixe. There is plenty of space at all of these, and they don't even get particularly busy in summer. The best of the bunch, however, is 🐾 *Praia Amoreira*, a 500-m stretch of sand that is enclosed by dramatic cliffs to the north (there is a path up to them next to the café). The Ribeira de Aljezur enters the wild Atlantic at the southern edge of the beach. It's a perfect spot for windswept walks or to spectate as surfers ride the waves.

AROUND ALJEZUR

5 ODECEIXE
16km north of Aljezur / 18 mins by car on the N 120

This charming village (pop. 950), with its inviting street cafés on the Largo 1 de Maio, is located at the northern-most point on the Algarve. From here, you need only cross the Rio Seixe to find yourself in Alentejo, which is well worth a visit – but first, head west, and after 2km you will reach one of the most beautiful beaches in Portugal. The enormous sandy expanse of the *Praia de Odeceixe* is flanked by steep cliffs; the Rio Seixe estuary forms a wonderful lagoon to swim in, and the beachfront cafés serve ice-cold white wine and fresh barnacles *(perceves)*. It's heaven on earth! If you decide to head into the village itself, *Restaurante Chaparro (closed Thu in winter | Rua Estrada National 8 | Tel. 2 82 94 73 04 | €€)* is a great spot for excellent seafood.

The pretty streets in the village are a pleasure to stroll around. As you explore, look out for the *Moinho de Odeceixe*, which should be on every-one's itinerary. The *Moinho* is one of numerous windmills that used to operate in this area – proof that this corner of Portugal has never been short of wind! It now operates as a small museum *(June–Sept Tue–Sat 10am–4.30pm | free admission | Serro da Igreja) | ⊞ D3*

Donkey-trekking is a fun way to explore the area

Golden sand and Atlantic surf at Praia da Bordeira

6 ARRIFANA ⭐

10km southwest of Aljezur / 13 mins by car on the M 1003-1

Set on a semi-circular bay, this chilled-out town is very popular with surfers. Head to the ruins of the 17th-century fort on the *Ponta da Arrifana* for magnificent views of crescent-shaped Arrifana bay and the striking coastline. It's the perfect spot for a picnic with a bottle of wine … especially when the sun is going down. If you don't want to take your own food, there is a good restaurant specialising in seafood right in front of the *fortaleza*, with big windows to take in the view: *Restaurante O Paulo (closed Mon | tel. 2 82 99 51 84 | restauranteopaulo. com | €€). | 🗺 C4*

7 CARRAPATEIRA

20km south of Aljezur / 20 mins by car on the N 120/N 268

This spot – nestled on the edge of green hills next to enormous, sandy *Praia da Bordeira* – is as endearing as they come. *Carrapateira* is part of the municipality of Bordeira, and taken together, the whitewashed houses of these two villages are home to 430 inhabitants. The small 16th-century *village church* offers great views over the picturesque settlement and its surroundings. Life here centres on the tiny market and the cafés surrounding it. The restaurant *Trigo Vermelho (closed Wed/Thu | Rua dos Quintais | tel. 2 82 97 39 08 | €)* prepares all of its dishes using local organic produce, most of it bought in the market.

Due to the natural fertility of the soil, traditionally more people in Carrapateira worked the land than the sea, although fishing was (and still is) regarded as an important side-line – which is why the locals are often referred to as "amphibians". You can find out all about their lives and livelihoods through the centuries at the *Museu do Mar e da Terra (Tue–Sat 10am–4.30pm | admission 2.70 euros | Rua do Pescador).*

The sea still plays a key role here today as you will be able to tell from the many happy surfers who stop in Carrapateira for an invigorating coffee after riding waves on ⚑ *Praia da Bordeira* and ⚑ *Praia do Amado (📖 C6)* to the south. Even if you're no surfer yourself, the atmosphere on Amado beach is pretty special: you can sit back and watch the wave-riders for hours!

A stunning section of the *Rota Vicentina* long-distance path passes through here, crossing the breathtakingly beautiful *Ponta de Carrapateira* headland. You'll get the best views of this rocky coastline if you walk between Carrapateira and Praia do Amado rather than driving along the dusty road as most visitors do.

INSIDER TIP
Spectacular cliffs all the way

There are plenty of other signposted hiking trails around Carrapateira and Bordeira, including some routes through the green hinterland. You will find fresh *perceves* – the "goose barnacles" that are so typical of this region – in lots of restaurants around here, but they are particularly good at *Sítio do Rio (closed Tue | Praia da Bordeira | tel. 2 82 97 31 19 | €). | 📖 C5–6*

WHERE TO SLEEP ON THE WEST COAST

TO THE MOON AND BACK

Despite its name – "height of the moon" – *Alto da Lua (Sítio Corte Pero Jaques | Espinhaço de Cão | Aljezur | tel. 282356047 | altodalua-algarve. com | €€–€€€)* is no lunar-themed hotel. Instead, you'll find a blissfully quiet guesthouse in the pine trees, with charming German hosts. From its perch on a 200-m-high plateau, it affords fabulous views out across a beautiful unspoiled landscape that continues as far as the Atlantic. The nine rooms are all south-facing, as is the pool terrace. It is about 20 minutes from here to the beaches at Carrapateira, the lights of Lagos or the tranquillity of Alzejur. And it takes little more than half an hour to reach the Serra de Monchique. In short, this gem is secluded without being remote. A hearty breakfast is provided, and there is also a communal kitchen, where you can make your own supper if you don't fancy driving into a local town. Afterwards, settle down in front of the fire in the cosy living room.

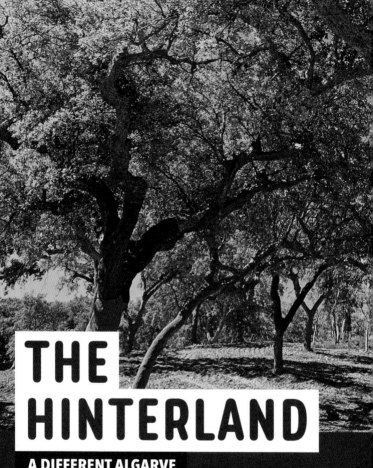

THE HINTERLAND

A DIFFERENT ALGARVE

When visitors think of the Algarve, they don't tend to summon up images of mountains and remote hillside villages, or of fertile valleys and cork plantations. It does not even occur to most holidaymakers to explore the area north of the A22 motorway. However, those that do will discover an altogether different side to the Algarve.

Cork oak forests provide shade in the Serra de Monchique

Even the three major towns here have nothing in common with the hustle and bustle of the coast. They are surrounded by wonderfully peaceful countryside that gives them a sense of remoteness. Rural traditions still characterise the "Garden of the Algarve", as this region is sometimes known. Hiking trails lead through a variety of hot and dry, or humid and fertile landscapes that offer a refreshing contrast to the densely populated areas along the coast.

THE HINTERLAND

Santa Clara-a-Velha

Santana da Serra

Barragem de Santa Clara

Pereiras

IC1

266

São Marcos da Serra

267

Medronho distillery
(Mata Porcas)

2

Monchique
p. 115

3 Fóia

4 Picota

Alferce

29 km, 8 hrs

S e r r a   d e   M o n c h i q u e

5 Caldas de Monchique ★

**Serra de
Monchique** ★

São Bartolomeu de Messines

A2

266

124

Canhestris

IC1

Mexilhoeira Grande

A22

Estômbar

Tunes

1 Algoz

Portimão

Parchal

Lagoa

Alcantarilha

Guia

Ferreira

Alvor

Ferragudo

125

Porches

Pêra

Carvoeiro

Armação de Pêra

Albufeira

Silves ★

p. 112

Santa Bárbara de Padrões

Rosário

Aldeia dos Fernandes

A2

Gomes Aires   Almodôvar

Santa Clara-a-Nova

São Barnabé

Ameixial

2

88km, 1½ hrs

50km, 40 mins

8 Rocha da Pena

6 Alte   124   **9** Salir

Benafim

7 Fonte Benémola

Tôr   Querença   2

Paderne   Alportel

São Brás de Alportel **10**

Boliqueime

A22   Loulé ★
p. 120

125   Santa Bárbara
de Nexe

Vale Formoso   4 km
2.49 mi

Almancil

MARCO POLO HIGHLIGHTS

★ **SILVES**
Take a trip back in time to the Moorish
era ➤ p. 112

★ **SERRA DE MONCHIQUE**
Cork trees and amazing views in the
Algarve's mountain range ➤ p. 115

★ **CALDAS DE MONCHIQUE**
Fairy-tale spa in a tiny valley ➤ p. 120

★ **LOULÉ**
Musical market town ➤ p. 120

Contemporary art in the historical capital of the Moors: market square in Silves

SILVES

(□ G 5–6) **The tranquil regional country town of ★ Silves (pop. 11, 000) – formerly known as Xelb and capital of the Moorish province of Al-Gharb – is a great place to track down what is left of the Moors and their rich culture. Or alternatively, just sit back in a café and enjoy the here and now!**

It is hard to imagine now that "Xelb" was once more important than Lisbon, and even comparable to Granada. A few remnants of the era of Moorish rule can be found in the archaeological museum and in the heavily restored castle, which glows bright red in the light of the sun. However, the town has changed a good deal since the Reconquista in the mid-13th century. This is partly due to the 1755 earthquake, but also because its main artery – the Rio Arade, which the Phoenicians once sailed up to access this part of the country, and which was the reason why the Moors established their capital here in the fertile, well-irrigated hinterland – has silted up. During low tide (that's right, the tide comes in all the way up to Silves!), the river is reduced to little more than a stream flowing under the town's beautiful five-arched 15th-century bridge.

Despite all these changes, Silves is a highly picturesque and charming little town, and it's fun to wander through its streets, climb up to the castle, browse through its shops or sit back in one of its charming cafés.

SIGHTSEEING

MUSEU MUNICIPAL DE ARQUEOLOGIA

Next to the city wall's erstwhile fortified tower, the *Torreão da Porta da Cidade*, you'll find the interesting *Archeological Museum*. Finds dating from the Stone Age era through to medieval times are exhibited here, including some beautiful Arabic ceramics. The descent into a 20-m deep Moorish well shaft, around which the museum was built, is spellbinding. *Daily 10am–6pm | admission 2.10 euros, combined ticket with the castelo 3.90 euros | Rua das Portas de Loulé 14*

SÉ

Below the castle looms the mid-13th-century cathedral – also built of red sandstone – which like so many churches was built on the ruins of the mosque. A few Gothic elements have been preserved despite severe damage during the 1755 earthquake, such as on the entrance portal, the choir and the crossing. *Mon–Fri 9am–5pm | admission 1 euro*

CASTELO

It's worth climbing to the top of the impregnable walls of the formerly Moorish fortress (8th–13th centuries) for the wonderful views alone, which take in the rooftops of the town and the surrounding orange groves. You can then walk from tower to tower along the top of the dark-red sandstone walls, which were a little over-zealously restored during the 1940s. Make sure you also head down into the enormous 13th-century cistern (which now houses an interesting exhibition about the Iberian lynx) and take a look at the (unfortunately rather scant) excavations of the former Moorish palace.

The cosy *café (€)* in the inner courtyard serves small snacks and delicious fruit juices. *Daily 9am–5.30pm. Stays open (much) later in summer | admission 2.80 euros, joint ticket with the Archaeological Museum 3.90 euros*

EATING & DRINKING

CAFÉ DAROSA

This venerable coffee house in the town hall has been charmingly restored. The blue and white *azulejos* on its walls have been scrubbed up so much you can almost see your face in them. Its cakes are superb – with the chocolate one the pick of the bunch. And the outside table are in a beautiful arcade. *Closed Sundays | Largo do Município 6 | Tel. 2 82 14 80 34 | FB: CafeDaRosa | €*

INSIDER TIP
A nostalgic coffee and dazzling tiles

CAFÉ INGLÊS

Enjoy a pizza, a salad or a slice of homemade cake in this lovely café. On Friday and Saturday evenings, as well as Sunday afternoons, you even get a side of live music. *Rua do Castelo 11 | tel. 2 82 44 25 85 | cafeingles.com.pt | €€*

O ALAMBIQUE

Marlen Schmid is the dedicated owner of this ultra-relaxed eatery in the Poço Barreto neighbourhood. We recommend her delicious dishes created using Algarve ingredients, or the international delicacies. Vegetarians will be happy here too! *Open evenings only, closed Tue | tel. 2 82 44 92 83 | FB: restaurante oalambiquesilves | €€–€€€*

O BARRADAS

Andrea Pequeno is a master chef while her husband Luís is a charming front of house expert. Their restaurant is a must if you want to have a delicious and elegant dinner in the Silves area. Try their fish baked in salt! *Evenings only, closed Wed | Venda Nova (2km to the south) | tel. 2 82 44 33 08 | obarradas.com | €€*

SPORT & ACTIVITIES

If you want to travel to Silves by boat up the *Rio Arade* – just like the Phoenicians did – then you can set sail with captain Adriano on the pleasure boat *"Cegonha do Arade" (departure times depend on the tides | 20 euros per trip | mobile tel. 9 14 98 39 67)* from the Largo do Dique in Portimão. There is also some great hiking by the *Barragem do Funcho* reservoir, 18km to the northeast of Silves. Near Algoz (see p. 115) 👤 *Krazy World petting zoo (daily 10am–6pm, in summer until 6.30pm, in winter until 5.30pm | admission 16.95 euros, children (4–10) 9.95 euros | krazyworld.com)* mainly pulls in a crowd made up of young families. The most entertaining critters are definitely the lemurs who splash around on the water slides!

Foia is the highest peak in the Algarve and provides the best views

BEACHES

There is a beautiful bathing area on a branch of the Rio Arade in the *Parque Municipal do Sítio das Fontes (between Silves and Estômbar, 7km to the southwest of Silves)*, which is particularly popular with local families. It's also a great spot for a picnic, and during the summer it has a real holiday atmosphere. But be warned, it does get extremely busy at the weekend!

AROUND SILVES

1 ALGOZ

14 km (8.5 miles) east of SIlves / 15 mins by car on the N 269

This tranquil provincial village – tucked away from the hustle and bustle –does not seem to have much to write home about at first. However, nearby on the road to Ferreiras you will find *Quinta dos Avós (Wed–Mon 2–7pm | quintadosavos.pt)* which specialises in traditional medieval monastic desserts and a variety of herbal teas. On Saturdays, the rural museum *Museu Rural* next door is open. ⌑ *J6*

MONCHIQUE

(⌑ F4) **Looking for some clear mountain air? Then head for the ★ Serra de Monchique, and make sure you take your walking boots with you! From the coastal villages around Portimão, it takes less than an hour to get to the highest peak in the Algarve, the 902-m Mount Fóia. The mountain town of Monchique is also well worth a visit.**

Monchique (pop. 4,800) has the atmosphere of a small village and is located around 460m up in the "groove" between the two main peaks of the mountain range. Its small streets run up hill, and its many cafés, bars and restaurants are good places to take a well-earned break if you have been exploring the Serra on foot. A lot of day-trippers just head to the summit of *Mount Fóia*, which offers some magnificent views on sunny days but is also spoilt by some aesthetically unappealing telecommunication masts.

However, the real appeal of the mountains will become apparent if you hike through cork oak forests to the top of *Picota* (773m), travel between the villages on a mountain bike, or get to know the region's flora on foot. The coastal mountains are blessed with over 1,000 different plant species. It's particularly worth visiting in spring, when the rock roses, wild orchids, camellias, azaleas and rhododendrons come into bloom. Despite a particularly bad year of forest fires in 2018, the countryside has recovered, and you will truly feel that you are in the garden of the Algarve.

You can also gain an impression of the landscape from your car. One particularly appealing drive runs down the N 267 from Monchique to

São Marcos da Serra, via Alferce. Alternatively, if you come from the south, there is a great route through the Ribeira de Odelouca's fertile valley: head out from Porto Lagos on the N 124 towards Silves, then turn left towards Barragem de Odelouca to eventually reach *Alferce (□ G4)*. En route, make sure you stop off at the *Barragem de Odelouca*, which is a great spot for a picnic. The reservoir here is one of the main water sources for the whole region.

> **INSIDER TIP**
> Detour for a dam good picnic

On the subject of water – the volcanic geology around Monchique means there are a lot of 🐗 natural springs (*fontes*) producing fresh drinking water. Do as the locals do and fill your bottles up whenever you see one!

SIGHTSEEING

IGREJA MATRIZ

This village church from the 15th/16th century is in daily use by the reverent residents of Monchique, while the tourists who visit come to see its extraordinary Manueline portal – it is surrounded by a twisted stone arc ending in massive knots (a typical feature of Manueline architecture). The chestnut wood altar has a statue of *Nossa Senhora da Conceição* dating from the 18th century.

NOSSA SENHORA DO DESTERRO

A short, well-signposted footpath starting in the town square (Largo dos Chorões) leads out through the narrow streets and into a cork oak forest to reach this Franciscan monastery, which was founded in 1631. There's not much left, since it was destroyed in the 1755 earthquake and subsequently abandoned, but there are beautiful views from here over Monchique.

EATING & DRINKING

As you drive up to the top of Mount Fóia, you will pass by a few rustic eateries that offer a good opportunity to stop for a break. It's also worth visiting the hilltop restaurant *Jardim das Oliveiras (Sítio do Porto Escuro | tel. 2 82 91 28 74 | jardimdasoliveiras. com | €€)*, which is signposted on the road up to Fóia. Surrounded by olive groves, this restaurant is famous for its hearty sausage and meat dishes (even wild boar). Monchique itself also boasts a number of good restaurants:

A CHARRETTE

Extremely relaxed with bags of Monchique ambiance and rustic charm. Wild boar, lamb stew, black pig and other Serra specialities. The menu is only available in Portuguese, but that can be an adventure in itself and good wines might help, too. *Closed Wed | Rua Dr. Samora Gil 30–34 | next to the town hall | tel. 2 82 91 21 42 | €€*

ÓCHÃLÁ

Head up the small pedestrianised street from the town square, Largo dos Chorões, to reach this friendly

Traditional crafts and traditional transport in Monchique

teahouse, which also serves delicious homemade pastries, sandwiches, salads and small vegetarian plates. *Closed Sun (also Sat in winter) | Rua Doutor Samora Gil 12 | tel. 2 82 91 25 24 | €*

SHOPPING

A variety of quality shops sell ceramics, wooden souvenirs, baskets and leather goods. Folding wooden chairs unique to the *serra* are a favourite tourist souvenir from the region (but require careful logistical planning to get them home). They are hand-crafted to a design that can be traced back to the Romans, suggesting that folding furniture isn't so new after all. Perhaps it's not surprising since the Romans were making good use of the

nearby hot springs at the resort of Caldas 2,000 years ago. The other thing to track down up here is *Medronho*, the locally produced spirit. The best place to get it is the *Loja de Mel e Medronho*, a proper booze shop founded when 50 local producers grouped together to sell their concoctions at a central point. Make sure to try before you buy – there is a considerable difference between the punchy *Medronho* and slightly sweeter *Melosa* (which has cinnamon and honey added to it).

SPORT & ACTIVITIES

The *serra* is a beautiful area for hiking and cycling – and a vast one. It has an endless network of roads, paths and trails that cover the Fóia and Picota

The fruit of the strawberry tree is the main ingredient in *Medronho*

mountains and the valleys, including the *Via Algarviana* hiking trail, which runs right through it. Cyclists who brave the 902-m climb up the Fóia will be rewarded with the thrill of coasting down the 35-km route to the sea. Motorists have to be very careful, especially on weekends when there are crowds of cyclists on the road. You can book a superb guided mountain bike tour from Mount Fóia to Mexilhoeira Grande (downhill for most of the route!) with the guys at *Outdoor Tours (outdoor-tours.com)*.

INSIDER TIP
Two-wheel tour

They'll provide the bikes, show you some beautiful spots in the Serra and even arrange a gloriously traditional lunch in Casais's village pub for you.

WELLNESS

There aren't many places in the Algarve where you can wallow in a hot spring but *Caldas de Monchique* (see p.120) fits the bill. Guests can relax in warm water (32°C) in the spa or enjoy a sauna, Vichy shower and a range of spa and beauty treatments in the surrounding hotels. All the facilities are centrally run and need to be booked online *(monchiquetermalresort.com)*. Alternatively, the nearby Macdonald *Monchique Resort & Spa (macdonald monchique.com)* offers massages.

AROUND MONCHIQUE

BARLEFANTE

Even the street leading up to this colourful, relaxed and alternative bar is worth seeing! Snacks are available, and live bands play here too from time to time. *Mon–Fri noon–2am, Sat 1pm–4am | Travessa das Guerreiras 14 | tel. 9 65 57 62 98 | FB: Barlefante | €*

FRIDAYHAPPINESS ASSOCIAÇÃO

This is a gloriously eccentric place. Volunteers run this hippyish farm and organise a legendary party every Friday night. At the *Pizzanight Algarve* you get all-you-can-eat homemade pizza as well as two drinks for 10 euros (!). The party goes on into the small hours with music and is always full of an interesting mix of people. *Fri from 6pm | Tojeiro | between Marmelete and the Autódromo | wp.friday happiness.org*

🖻 MEDRONHO DISTILLERY

2km north of Monchique / around 5 mins by car on the M 501

Once you've tried a glass of 🏳 medronho you may want to learn more about this regional spirit. In which case, pay a visit to Senhor António *(tel. 2 82 91 27 10)* and his distillery near the hamlet of Mata Porcas. He also makes honey which he puts to excellent use in the significantly sweeter *melosa* (*medronho* + honey + cinnamon). You will find both of these in supermarkets, but they're often produced using industrial processes. Senhor António's drinks taste significantly better. *📖 F4*

INSIDER TIP
Just a tiny sip …

MEDRONHO – STRAWBERRY JUICE FOR GROWN-UPS

Medronho is distilled from the ripe fruits of the strawberry tree and doesn't actually have anything to do with strawberries aside from its bright colour. In the autumn, local farmers painstakingly harvest its fruit up in the mountains, as the *medron-heiro* can't be cultivated in orchards. Around 8kg of fruit are needed to produce just one litre of fiery spirit in the spring. In other words, it's hard work out in the fields …. And in the distillery too as the *aguardente de medronho* needs to flow evenly out of the still so the temperature needs to be kept constant. This means fires burning day and night, and whole families (often with neighbours) helping out, until the wooden barrels that the fruits have spent the whole winter fermenting in are finally empty and the bottles are full. Not everybody who distils this brandy at home has a licence to do so, but the authorities will often turn a blind eye in order to preserve the tradition.

3 FÓIA

8km west of Monchique / 15 mins by car on the N 266-3

After the captivating drive from Monchique, you know you have reached the summit when you can see the disconcerting array of aerials and radar units on the 902-m-high plateau. Despite this modern infrastructure, the view from here is sensational! Throw on a jacket as it can get quite windy. Deserted farms and villages and the remnants of painstaking terracing bear silent testimony to a once thriving agricultural lifestyle.

When driving down, after 2km stop at the *Miradouro da Fonte Santa* to the right, where you'll find a 🐷 spring (*fonte*) where you can get some cool, fresh mountain water. *⊞ F4*

4 PICOTA

4km east of Monchique / around 1 hr on foot

The view from this 773-m-high granite peak is perhaps even more stunning than that from Fóia. On a clear day you will be able to see the entire coastline and the magnificent Alentejo region. You can get to the top via a dirt track signposted from the road to Alferce; however, it's much nicer to climb Picota via the well-marked *Via Algarviana* trail (around 6km there and back), which leads through some wonderful cork oak forests (most of which escaped the 2018 forest fires). *⊞ F4*

5 CALDAS DE MONCHIQUE ⭐

5km south of Monchique / 8 mins by car on the N 266

These spring waters have been attracting visitors since the Romans started using them to cure rheumatism, skin disorders and respiratory illnesses. Today, the belle époque-style buildings have been restored and new buildings added to create a beautiful small resort. Two million litres of water a day bubble up from the thermal springs, some of which is bottled and sold as *Água de Monchique* throughout Portugal. Those who don't fancy spending the night here can still enjoy a stroll, taking in the fresh air and romantic atmosphere of the resort. Good food can be had at *Wine & Beer Bar O Tasco* (tel. *2 82 91 09 13 | €*) and the smarter *Restaurante 1692* (tel. *2 82 91 09 10 | €€€*) where you can sit outside under its shady trees. *⊞ F4*

LOULÉ

(⊞ L6) **A town that loves to party! Loulé's population makes the most of any opportunity for a celebration. It is one of the most important carnival towns in Portugal and, after Easter, the religious festival Mãe Soberana fills the streets with processions and onlookers. In the summer, the annual MED World Music Festival offers a more secular reason to celebrate, with stages placed all around the old town.**

But even without a festival, ⭐ Loulé (pop. 20 000) is a charming small town to visit. It is a place best explored on foot – take some time to stroll through the pretty, narrow

The Festa da Mãe Soberana is one of many important festivals in Loulé

streets in the old town, with their relics from the Moorish era, before browsing in some of the delightful shops here. After that, make sure you pay a visit to the *market hall*. With its onion domes and horseshoe arches, this neo-Moorish building – opened in 1908 – can't fail to catch the eye of all who pass it. Yet it's the interior that will really blow you away: crowds bustle around enticingly laid-out stalls selling not only fruit, vegetables, bread and fish, but a large selection of handicrafts, regional products and other popular souvenirs. The fact that the market hall is the town's most impressive building is clear from its prominent position directly on Loulé's main street, next door to the old town hall. Behind it, the streets of the old town lead off towards the church or the castle. This is

the heart of the former Moorish settlement of Al-Ulyá – "the higher up" – so-called because Loulé is situated on the fertile hills of the Barrocal.

SIGHTSEEING

OLD TOWN

In reality this only consists of two or three streets that lead from the castle to the church, but they are so picturesque that you'll find any excuse to stroll up and down them more than once. At the northern end of the small *centro histórico*, opposite the castle, the ☛ *Nossa Senhora da Conceição (closed Sun/Mon | admission free)* is worth a look – not only for its beautiful *azulejos* and 18th-century gilded wood

INSIDER TIP
Terrific tiles

A street in Loulé's old town covered with colourful sun shades

carving but also for the remains of the Moorish city wall that are displayed underneath the glass floor.

A little further along, on the cosy *Largo Dom Pedro I*, archaeologists have been working for years to unearth a Moorish hammam – and sometimes they leave the door open so you can watch them work. You can also find traces of the town's Islamic heritage at the *Igreja de São Clemente* parish church at the southern end of the old town: Christians built this 13th-century church on top of the old mosque (as was so often the case) and used the minaret as the bell-tower. Across the way, on the site of what used to be a Moorish cemetery, you can relax under the monkey puzzle trees in the adorable *Jardim dos Amuados*.

CASTELO & MUSEU DE LOULÉ

Parts of the 12th-century former Moorish castle are now home to Loulé's municipal museum, which is worth visiting for one key reason: you can climb the towers of the castle and view the town from above! It also houses an interesting archaeological exhibition (with Roman amphorae and ceramics), as well as a fully furnished farmer's kitchen from the mid-20th century. *Tue–Fri 9.30am5.30pm (10am-6pm in summer), Sat 9.30am-4pm (10am-4.30pm in summer) | admission 1.62 euros | Rua D. Paio Peres Correia 17 | museudeloule.pt*

NOSSA SENHORA DA PIEDADE

The modern pilgrims' church perched on a hill a little to the west of the town looks a bit like a UFO and makes the neighbouring Renaissance chapel (built in 1553) look rather insubstantial. The latter was much too small to accommodate the annual *Festa da Mãe Soberana* – one of the biggest Marian celebrations in Portugal. Every year eight strong local mean haul a 360kg statue of the Virgin Mary down from here to the Franciscan church for the start of this festival. Two weeks later, they have to drag it all the way back as the celebrations reach their peak. For reasons probably best known to them, the men carry the holy relic in a monkey cage.

EATING & DRINKING

BOCAGE

This place looks completely unprepossessing from the outside, and the interior is rather plain too – but the food is genuinely superb! Traditional Algarve dishes are served here without any frills, and there are cheap lunch menus too. Reservation recommended – and with good reason! *Closed Sun | Rua Bocage 14 | tel. 28 90 41 24 16 | restaurantbocage. com | €€*

CAFÉ CALÇINHA

Born illiterate, António Aleixo went on to become a politically engaged but romantic poet, well-known throughout Portugal. His presence, immortalised in bronze, still graces the entrance to his favourite café 70 years after his death. The café itself has recently been restored but has retained its refined European coffee-house flair. Alongside coffee and cake, it serves hearty snacks and even heartier main courses. The café hosts readings, fado performances and piano concerts some evenings. *Daily | Praça da República | el. 2 89 46 23 30 | FB: cafecalcinha | €*

INSIDER TIP Coffee, cake and culture

MUSEU DO LAGAR

This rustic restaurant next door to the parish church was formerly an olive oil mill and still retains its millstone and much of its equipment, so the name *"museu"* isn't far off the mark. You can dine on exquisite grilled meat dishes here, including pork from black Iberian pigs. There is also live music some evenings. *Closed Sun | tel. 9 69 53 69 25 | FB: museudolagar | €€*

SHOPPING

All great shopping experiences in Loulé revolve around the grand *covered market (Mon–Sat 7am–3pm)*. It is great place to pick up hand-crafted and culinary delights. On Saturday mornings there is an additional weekly market in the area around the main hall. There are nice little shops in the pedestrian precinct *Rua 5 de Outubro*. Carefully hand-painted ceramics can be found at *Teresa's Pottery (Largo Dom Pedro I 15 | teresapottery.com)* in the historic centre.

AROUND LOULÉ

6 ALTE

25km northwest of Loulé / 30 mins by car on the N 124

Fig and orange groves surround the village. Charming squares, natural springs, a brook, narrow streets and beautiful balcony balustrades decorated with hanging baskets in a myriad of colours all give Alte a traditional rural atmosphere. The village is also well known for its astonishingly excessive carnival celebrations (but you may not believe this if you visit at other times of the year). *K5*

7 FONTE DA BENÉMOLA

10km north of Loulé / 15 mins by car on the EM 525

Fonte da Benémola is a stunning, tranquil rural area containing a multitude of natural springs. It is a great place for a picnic or a walk – with a 4.5-km circular trail that leads hikers around the area. On the way to the car park at the head of the trail, you will pass *Querença*, a sweet village that is worth a stop. Take a stroll to the pretty church square with its village cafés. *M5*

8 ROCHA DA PENA

21km north of Loulé / 30 mins by car on the EM 525

Incredible cliffs and boulders, 120 species of bird and 500 different plants: the best way to get a sense of this natural paradise is a circular walk.

Start at the *Bar das Grutas* at the base of the plateau and start climbing. You need to ascend 200m to reach the top of the plateau at 485m. Head to the northern edge for a stunning view over the Serra do Caldeirão. After that, just walk around – there are stunning

Take a short break in the churchyard of Barranco do Velho

views in every direction from up here. Head back after exploring the hamlet of Penina (and its small pub). *K5*

🟑 SALIR

15km north of Loulé / 20 mins by car on the EM 525

Salir is a typical village in the Algarve hinterland. Of the Moorish fort on a hill, all that is visible today are the remnants of a few walls. The area around the hill was occupied as far back as 4,000 years ago. A scenic route on the N 124 takes you from the fort (keep a look out for eagles that circle over the cork oak and eucalyptus groves) to *Barranco do Velho*, which is over the regional border in the Serra do Caldeirão. If you have time, it is far more pleasant to walk this route along stage 6 of the *Via Algarviana*. If you start in Barranco and head back to Salir, it is even downhill! *(15km, approx. 5 hours walking). L5*

🔟 SÃO BRÁS DE ALPORTEL

13km east of Loulé / 18 mins by car on the N 270

This small and quite provincial town (pop. 10,700) has two great indoor attractions – making it ideal for any rainy days. The first is the *Novacortiça* cork factory *(1½-hr tour can be booked online | 12.50 euros | Parque Industrial da Barracha | novacortica.pt)*, which offers guided tours to explain how tree bark is converted into bottle stops (and a host of other products). It is also well worth paying a visit to the town's small museum, the 🎭 *Museu do Traje (Mon–Fri 10am–1pm and 2–5pm, Sat/Sun 2–5pm | admission 2 euros | Rua Dr. José Dias Sancho 61 | museu-sbras. com)*. The beating cultural heart of the town, it has a constantly changing set of exhibitions and events, a nice café and a courtyard full of beautiful historic carriages. *N6*

WHERE TO SLEEP IN THE HINTERLAND

YOGA, PEACE, RELAXATION

Fancy the idea of stargazing from the comfort of a warm jacuzzi in a beautiful garden? The relaxed atmosphere at *The Art of Joy (Caminho da Fóia | Monchique | Tel. 9 11 05 86 33 | theartofjoy.nl | €€)*, an eco-lodge where sustainability and mindfulness are placed front and centre, makes it the perfect place to escape to on holiday. Its Dutch owners, Anne and Eus are welcoming and extremely attentive, which means the whole place is a wonderfully relaxing and rejuvenating place to be. It is set a good 4km outside Monchique – isolation and contemplation are very much the order of the day. There are only two B&B rooms and two apartments but the small number of guests here do get great views down to the coast. Your hosts also offer guided walks, breathing workshops and life coaching. Each year they organise a few special walking weeks (sometimes combined with yoga). The guesthouse is open from March to October.

DISCOVERY TOURS

Want to get under the skin of the region? Then our discovery tours provide the perfect guide – they include advice on which sights to visit, tips on where to stop for that perfect holiday snap, a choice of the best places to eat and drink and suggestions for fun activities

① AT ONE WITH NATURE: THE WILD WEST

➤ The natural world in all its rugged, untouched beauty
➤ Spectacular views from Europe's most southwesterly point
➤ Plenty of opportunities to swim at remote beaches

📍	Lagos	🏁	Salema
🚗	Distance: 130km	→	1 day (4½ hrs total driving time)

ℹ️ Allow 60–80 euros per person, including car hire, petrol and food
Caution: on some sections (most notably beach access roads) you will have to drive very slowly.

Praia da Bordeira will be a highlight of your tour

DELICIOUS BISCUITS ON THE WAY TO A RUINED FORT

From ❶ Lagos ➤ p. 68 *take the N 120 northwest towards Bensafrim* and you will soon encounter fertile agricultural land in varying shades of green occasionally interrupted by dots of orange and yellow from citrus fruit trees – definitely a stark contrast to the Algarve's coast! Pass through Bensafrim after which the N 120 takes you up and down through scrub land and past eucalyptus, pine and cork trees until you meet the main road from Sagres on your left – your first destination for today is ❷ Aljezur ➤ p. 102. Park up on the patch of gravel beyond the bridge on the right directly opposite the covered market. Make sure to pick up some *Delicias de Aljezur* here, small biscuits which come in almond, sweet potato or carob varieties. You are best off exploring the historical part of Aljezur on foot. Start by crossing the bridge and then head up to the fortress through the narrow streets. You get amazing views of the sea from up here. As this name implies, Aljezur was once a Moorish town and this was their lookout.

❶ Lagos
32.5km 13mins

❷ Aljezur
8.5km 48mins

INSIDER TIP
Brilliant biccies

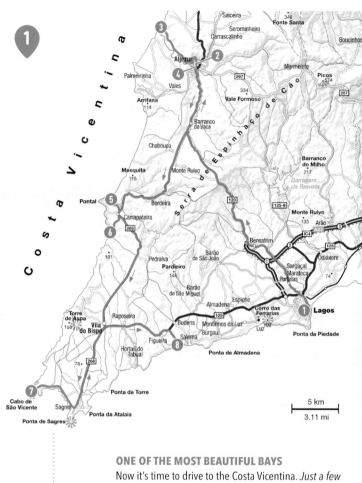

ONE OF THE MOST BEAUTIFUL BAYS

Now it's time to drive to the Costa Vicentina. *Just a few kilometres northwest of Aljezur*, the ❸ Praia da Amoreira (signposted turnoff) stretches out and is admired by both locals and visitors as one of Portugal's most captivating bays on the west coast. Don't miss the chance to dive into the Atlantic here! Splashing around in the water will have woken an appetite in you, so after this short detour to the beach, jump back in the car and head on to ❹ Pont'a Pé ➤ p. 104, a nearby trendy restaurant. Almost every dish on the menu is served with local sweet potatoes.

❸ **Praia da Amoreira**
9km 15mins

❹ **Pont'a Pé**
21.5km 23mins

A LAGOON & A STROLL WITH A VIEW

After your meal, *take the N 268 heading south from Aljezur* through a sparsely populated region. You will reach Bordeira on your left but carry on to the next town of Carrapateira ➤ p. 106. *Take a right down to* ❺ Praia da Bordeira, where sand dunes separate a lagoon from the sea. Take advantage of the proximity to one of the Algarve's best long-distance paths and take a stroll on the *Rota Vicentina*. From the path, you will get great views of the beach below. You can theoretically carry on to the next beach (about 7km). Quite a lot of people also drive on this dirt track, but save the walkers a cloud of dust and *hit the proper road again before heading to the* ❻ Praia do Amado, a beach much loved by surfers.

❺ Praia da Bordeira
4km 9mins

❻ Praia do Amado
30km 35mins

A LIGHTHOUSE & FRESH FISH

Back on the main road, drive through Vila do Bispo and the port town of Sagres ➤ p. 98 to ❼ Cabo de São Vicente ➤ p. 101. The rugged coastal panorama around the lighthouse is unrivalled. If you are hungry here, pick up a sausage from the German sausage stand. Finish your tour by *driving off the N 125 for a last detour to Portugal's southern coast.* Your destination is ❽ Salema with its splendid beach. Slowly unwind by taking a dip in the Atlantic or a bite to eat in one of the town's bars and restaurants like A Boia ➤ p. 76, which offers a special location and serves great seafood.

❼ Cabo de São Vicente
24km 24mins

❽ Salema

Tourist honeypot: Cabo de São Vicente

❷ HISTORY & CULTURE ON THE BORDER: THE UNDISCOVERED EAST

➤ Beautiful drive along the Rio Guadina
➤ Take a detour to Alentejo and travel back to the Moorish period
➤ Brave the border in Alcoutim

📍 Castro Marim

🏁 Vila Real de Santo António

🚗 Distance: 160km

➡ 1 day (3½ hrs total driving time)

ℹ Allow 80 euros per person, including rental car, fuel, food, admissions, ferry (2 euros), zip line (18 euros/pers)
Don't forget your binoculars!
Note that tourist sites in Mértola are closed on Mondays; reserve a zip line at *mobile tel. 0034 670 313 933* or*limitezero.com*

❶ Castro Marim
37.5km 52mins

TIME TRAVEL IN THE CASTELO

Let the time travel commence! Start this tour with a visit to ❶ Castro Marim ➤ p. 61, 6km to the north of Vila Real. You will spot the castelo perching on a hill from some distance away. It is well worth a visit and takes you high up to the town. The castle was home to the influential Military Order of Christ back in the 14th century is crying out for you to conquer it! It's a long (sweaty slog up) but you will be rewarded with stunning views over the Rio Guadiana lowlands and the Reserva Natural do Sapal de Castro Marim ➤ p. 62 where you may be able to see the flamingos frolicking.

SOME CHILLED OUT TWITCHING BEFORE A HIGH-OCTANE BORDER CROSSING

After visiting the castle, *head north on the N 122 (IC 27). Approximately 12km after Castro Marim, turn right to Foz de Odeleite taking the riverside road along the wide*

and tidal Rio Guadiana ➤ p. 60. The views from this road are incredible!! This river, which marks the border to Spain, is 744km long yet only the last 50km stretch before its estuary is navigable. The neighbouring valleys are home to many species of birds, some of which are rare and endangered. Take a longer break in ❷ Alcoutim ➤ p. 63 where you can take advantage of perhaps the most James Bond border crossing in Europe! Instead of checkpoints and traffic jams, here you can fly across to Spain on a zipline! Limitezero *(daily in the summer 10am–2pm and 4–8pm, otherwise Wed–Sun 10:30am–2pm and 3–7pm. They are based in Spain, so all times are in Spanish time – one hour later than Portugal)* are the people who can make this happen for you. The zip line is over 700m long and reaches maximum speeds of 80kmh. The line starts in Sanlúcar de Guadiana on the Spanish side – which you can reach by a frequent ferry – the journey only lasts approximately three minutes. Anyone who thinks the zipline may be too high octane can spend some (sedate) time visiting the secluded castelo in Alcoutim. The village square has a few decent lunch spots but O Camané is one of the best. *(daily | €)*.

INSIDER TIP
Zip across the border

HISTORY THAT WILL HAVE YOU COMING BACK FOR MOOR

After lunch, get back in the car and drive through a virtually uninhabited region before reaching the Alentejo. The castle of ❸ Mértola suddenly appears in front of you. Narrow streets wind between small whitewashed houses up to the parish church of Igreja Matriz. There is nowhere else in the Algarve where the presence of Islamic Portugal can be so keenly felt as here with its

❷ Alcoutim
37km 36mins

❸ Mértola
70.5km 64mins

A peaceful destination at the end of an exciting day: Vila Real de Sant António

hoof-shaped entrance and Islamic mihrab facing Mecca. However the town's highlight is its castle and its imposing tower, the Torre de Menagem. Enjoy the view and then a refreshment in one of the cafés in the lower part of town.

RESERVOIR REST AND THEN AN ATMOSPHERIC WAY TO END THE DAY

Now head *south from Mértola on the N 122 (IC 27)* directly back to Vila Real de Santo António without any more major detours. On the last section of this route, you'll notice on your right the reservoir (Barragem) of Odeleite. Before winding down the day here, first drive along this partly bumpy road *for a few kilometres*

following the river until you reach a turnoff to the right, at the end of which is the car park for the ❹ Praia de Santo António – a vast stretch of beach unknown to many tourists which extends almost to the mouth of the Rio Guadiana and is surrounded by sand dunes. After a spot of (sun) bathing, take a stroll around the historical centre of ❺ Vila Real de Santo António ➤ p. 59 before the pangs of hunger start to get too loud. There are lots of good places to sate them on the main square but one that it is popular with locals and tourists alike is Puro Café *(daily | Rua 5 de Outubro 13 | tel. 2 81 51 24 99 | €).*

❹ **Praia de Santo António**

4.5km 10mins

❺ **Vila Real de Santo António**

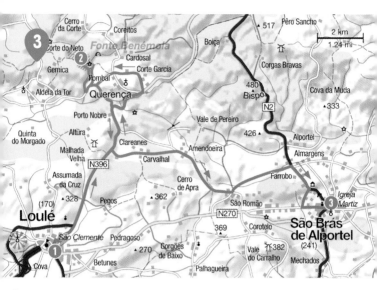

❸ THROUGH THE UNSPOILT HINTERLAND

➤ Food shopping in the Algarve's most beautiful covered market
➤ A circular walk to a refreshing natural spring
➤ Cork and culture in sleepy small places

📍 Loulé		🏁	São Brás de Alportel
🚗 Distance: 30km		→	7 hours, including a 1-hour walk

ℹ️ Allow 20 euros per person, including food and admissions
What to pack: hiking shoes, water to drink, food and snacks
Important tip: don't forget sunscreen for the hike in summer (and headwear)

❶ Loulé
14.5km   30mins

SENSORY STIMULATION TO START TO THE DAY

Start in ❶ Loulé ➤ p. 120. Let yourself get lost among the fresh bread, flowers, figs and fish at the market and make sure to stock up on supplies for your hike later. You will still have some time left over for a stroll through the town to visit the castelo. If this wander puts you in the mood for a second breakfast, Café Calcinha *(Praça da República | FB: Café Calcinha | €)* is an ideal place to chill out before getting in the car.

WALK THROUGH LUSH COUNTRYSIDE

Suitably stuffed, jump in the car and *set off in a north-easterly direction to Querença where you then follow the signs* to the small 392-hectare natural reserve of ❷ Fonte da Benémola. The circular route is signposted with yellow and red markings. The route is about 4.5km in total. It should not be too strenuous – and you will be grateful (especially in summer) that *you mostly follow a lush green valley*. Once you reach the babbling Benémola spring, it will be time to stop and tuck into your picnic in the shade of the many trees here. After a decent rest (don't forget to fill your water bottles), *simply cross the crystal-clear water using the concrete bollards and head back to your car on the other side of the river*.

❷ Fonte da Ben

17.5km 30mins

CULTURAL IMMERSION

Continue on the N 396 and the N 2 until you reach the old cork town of ❸ São Brás de Alportel ➤ p. 125, which is still home to a handful of cork factories today. You'll arrive in the afternoon just when the Museu do Traje ➤ p. 125 is open. This is not your typical, dusty local museum specialising in traditional folk dress but rather a cultural centre which regularly also hosts interesting events. An interesting side wing is dedicated to the extraction and production of cork and its courtyard houses a collection of historic carriages. The museum's bar with its delightful summer terrace is the perfect way to end your day trip.

❸ São Brás de Alportel

Loulé market is a riot of colour and a feast for the senses

GOOD TO KNOW

HOLIDAY BASICS

ARRIVAL

GETTING THERE

It is possible to drive or take the train from the UK to the Algarve if you have the time and the stamina – both of these options will take up to two days. Less green, but cheaper and easier, is to take advantage of the huge number of flights from various UK airports to Faro. Depending on the point of departure, the flight takes about 2½ hours and is offered by virtually every major airline. Prices vary and booking early is advisable, especially if you intend to go in the summer.

All the information you could possibly need about Faro airport is online at *ana.pt*. On arrival, once you have got through all the formalities, you will find a large range of car hire companies in the Arrivals Hall. There are also always lots of taxis in the rank just outside the terminal building. To get to the centre of the city, you have two options: take a taxi, which should cost around 15 euros and can be pre-booked online *(aeroportodefaro.com/taxis)*, or take a no. 14 or no. 16 bus (2.35 euros), although the buses only depart at irregular intervals, mostly just once an hour. The bus stop is by the short-stay car park, opposite the taxi rank – the one with the *Próximo (proximo.pt)* timetable. Both buses go to the central bus station in the city

Portugal uses GMT (and clocks change on the same dates as in the UK), so it is always the same time in the Algarve as in the UK and Ireland.

Discover beautiful natural landscapes, such as the Rio Formosa

centre, from where you can easily change buses to reach every corner of the Algarve.

If you want to combine a trip to the Algarve with a city break in Lisbon, you can fly directly to Lisbon, spend two days in the capital and then take a bus or train to the south. The train from Lisbon to Lagos takes about four hours with one change and should cost a little over 20 euros if booked in advance. There are also a range of bus options from Lisbon's main bus stations to all the major destinations in the Algarve, taking about three hours and costing around 20 euros.

GETTING IN

UK and other non-EU citizens do not need to apply for a visa for visits of up to 90 days. For longer trips, check the Portuguese embassy homepage. EU citizens can travel freely to Portugal with no restrictions on length of stay.

RESPONSIBLE TRAVEL

It doesn't take a lot to be environmentally friendly while travelling. Don't just think about your carbon footprint while flying to and from your holiday destination, but also about how you can protect nature and culture abroad. As a tourist, it is especially important to respect nature, look out for local products, cycle instead of driving, save water and much more. If you would like to find out more about eco-tourism please visit: www.ecotourism.org.

CLIMATE & WHEN TO GO

Europe's most southwesterly region lies on the Atlantic Ocean but has a mild Mediterranean climate and does not get snow in the winter. During the summer months between May and October it can get particularly hot.

Check the chart (p. 143) for a sense of the weather when you are going, but generally it is wise to pack a jumper or jacket for cooler evenings. It practically never rains in summer, although showers may occur during transition periods between the seasons, so it's worth packing a light raincoat.

GETTING AROUND

CAR HIRE & DRIVING
For the best prices, book in advance and compare prices between providers. You have to be 21 years of age to hire a car or motorbike, and you'll usually need your passport, driving licence and a credit card. All major car hire companies have branches at Faro airport; some will bring your car directly to your hotel. If you want to drive on the A 22 motorway, you will need a toll calculator with your car hire (normally around 2 euros a day), which works out your toll fees automatically. Tolls here are complicated, so to work out how much you will be charged, refer to an online calculator (such as on Google Maps). Speed limits for cars are 50kph in urban areas, 90kph on open roads and 120kph on motorways. EU blood alcohol limits apply: 0.5g of alcohol per litre of blood (or 0.2g for some drivers).

PUBLIC TRANSPORT
All the bigger destinations in the Algarve are well served by buses, both within individual towns and between them. You can travel by bus from the Algarve to Lisbon in about three hours; it's not expensive. For timetables and tickets, check the website of the company that operates on the route you want to take (eva-bus.com, frotazul-algarve.pt, rede-expressos.pt).

The Algarve coast between Lagos and Vila Real de Santo António is well served by trains too (cp.pt). Some stretches, such as the one that runs from Faro to Tavira past the lagunas of the Ria Formosa, are stunningly beautiful. The stations in Faro, Tavira, Portimão and Lagos are in the middle of town; the station for Albufeira is Ferreiras, which is 5km from town.

INSIDER TIP
Take the train

TAXI
The taxi metre will show the exact fare. There are surcharges for suitcases and late-night/weekend trips.

EMERGENCIES

CONSULATES & EMBASSIES
British Consulate in Portimão
Largo Francisco A Mauricio 7-1 | 8500-355 Portimao | Faro | tel. 2 82 49 07 50 | gov.uk/government/world/organisations/british-embassy-lisbon
United States Embassy in Lisbon
Av. das Forças Armadas | Sete-Rios | 1600-081 | Lisbon | tel. 2 17 70 21 22 | portugal.usembassy.gov/service.html

FESTIVALS & EVENTS
ALL YEAR ROUND

FEBRUARY
Carnival (Alte, Loulé, Moncarapacho, Monte Gordo, Paderne and others)

MARCH/APRIL
Festa da Mãe Soberana (Loulé): the Algarve's biggest religious festival begins with a grand Easter procession.

MAY
Festival Islâmico (Mértola/Alentejo only in odd years): Islamic Festival. *festivalislamicodemertola.com*

JUNE
Santos Populares (all over): devoted to the most popular patron saints. Large processions in Santo António, São Pedro and São João.
Festival MED (Loulé): top-class world music in the narrow streets of the old town. *festivalmed.pt*

JULY
Festa dos Pescadores: (Arrifana) big festival of fishing, held at the same time as **Arrifana Sunset Fest** *(arrifana sunsetfest.com)* with lots of live music.

AUGUST
Feira Medieval (Silves): medieval market. FB: Feira Medieval de Silves
Festival do Marisco (Olhão): seafood festival with concerts. *festivaldo marisco.com*
Festival da Sardinha (Portimão): sardine festival with lots of music. *cm-portimao.pt/festivaldasardinha*
Dias Medievais (Castro Marim): "Medieval Days". *diasmedievais.cm-castromarim.pt*
Festival F (Faro): music festival in the old town. *festivalf.pt*

OCTOBER
Birdwatching Festival (Sagres). *birdwatchingsagres.com*

NOVEMBER
Festival da batata doçe (Aljezur): sweet potato festival. *festival-batata-doce.cm-aljezur.pt*

EMERGENCY SERVICES

Call 112 for police, fire brigade and ambulance.

HEALTH

Ensure you have comprehensive healthcare cover in your travel insurance. Good insurance should cover treatment in the accident and emergency department *(urgências)* of local GP clinics *(centros de saúde)* or state-run hospitals *(hospital)*. Some insurance will allow you to be treated by a private hospital or a doctors' practice where waiting times will be shorter and where English is also often spoken. You may, however, have to pay your bill upfront so it is imperative that you keep all treatment and medication invoices.

Pharmacies *(farmácias)* are useful for any prescription-only medication but, as in the UK, lots of basic medication can be procured off the shelf in supermarkets.

ESSENTIALS

ACCOMMODATION

There is an extraordinary range of options in the Algarve, from campsites to the poshest luxury hotels with plenty of youth hostels *(pousadas juventude.pt)* and B&Bs in between.

The highest hotel concentration is in the Barlavento, especially in the areas around Albufeira, Armação de Pêra and Portimão (where it could be argued that they have ruined a beautiful stretch of coast). Carvoeiro and Lagos have not been swallowed up to the same extent, while Sagres and its surrounding area is well served by smaller places.

The hotels around Vilamoura and in the "Golden Triangle" around Quinta do Lago are often fairly smart. Faro, Olhão and Tavira have plenty of good places to stay without being overrun. Monte Gordo is the place in the Sotavento most subsumed by mass tourism.

The hinterland and the west coast have very few large hotels. Here you will find a number of lovely smaller places and holiday lets.

BEACHES

The Atlantic is not the Mediterranean and can be subject to dangerous currents and undertows, so the safety flags on beaches really are worth taking into consideration. Blue flags don't tell you anything about the conditions – they mean that the beach itself is particularly clean. It is also worth being aware of signs warning about falling rocks/unstable cliffs. Every year there are fatal accidents on the Algarve caused by its rocky coastline. Those used to the UK/Irish coast will not be surprised by the tidal difference on the Algarve, which can be several metres at different times of day *(tide tables at hidrografico.pt/previsao-maresfaro.php)*.

Nudism is only allowed on a small number of beaches – Adegas near Odeceixe, Deserta near Faro and Barril near Tavira – but topless sunbathing is more widely accepted.

CAMPING

You will find campsites all over the Algarve – they are very often in excellent locations (just outside village centres or at the beach). You will see a lot of campervans from all over Europe in the Algarve. For information on where they can be accommodated and for the best campsites, refer to *camping.info and autocaravan algarve.com*. Wild camping is illegal in Portugal, as is parking up a campervan in a non-official car park. Some places (mainly Sagres and Aljezur) are enforcing these rules with ever greater rigour. Use the websites above to avoid being moved on and/or fined.

CUSTOMS

Visitors from the UK and other countries outside the EU customs union are subject to limits on the import and export of goods as follows: 200 cigarettes, 250 g tobacco, 1 litre of spirits (over 22 % vol.), 2 litres of spirits (under 22 % vol.), 2 litres of any wine. If you are at all worried about what you are bringing in, check online for up-to-date limits.

DRINKING WATER

Tap water on the coast can taste of chlorine but is safe. In the hinterland, it is beautifully clear and tastes great. You can, of course, buy bottled water in supermarkets if you are at all worried.

INFORMATION

The websites of the national and regional tourist associations, *visit portugal.com* and *visitalgarve.com*,

Olhão's picturesque fishing quarter

provide all kinds of useful information.

The Algarve's cities and bigger towns all have their own centrally located tourist information office *(posto de turismo)*, where you can get city maps, hiking brochures and more.

LANGUAGE

Unsurprisingly, Portuguese is the language spoken in the Algarve, but you will get by with English in virtually all contexts on the coast. (It is not worth practising your school Spanish; even though it is often understood in Portugal, people can be insulted by its use). In some places in the hinterland, you will have to resort to gestures!

MARKETS

Every city has a regional market or *mercado municipal* where fresh fruit, vegetables, meat and fish can be bought. Generally open Monday to Saturday 8am–1pm, the best of these are in Loulé and Olhão. Aside from these, all the districts *(concelhos)* hold a flea market once a month.

MONEY

The euro is Portugal's currency. There are ATMs everywhere *(multibanco)*. Be aware that your banks may charge fees and that lots of Portuguese banks will limit you to a maximum of two 200-euro withdrawals a day. Virtually everywhere takes credit cards but having a little cash for the exceptions is a good policy, especially in remoter places.

OPENING HOURS

Many restaurants tend to be closed on either Sunday or Monday in the winter months. In summer most restaurants are open all week. As a rule, shops are open Monday to Friday 10am–1pm and 3–7pm, Saturday until 1pm. Big supermarkets are open seven days a week, mostly 9am–10pm. Museums and places of interest are often closed on a Monday and/or Sunday. Some museums and other institutions change their opening hours up to five times a year so checking online before planning a visit is always a good idea.

POST

Post offices *(CTT or correios)* are red and are open Monday to Friday 8am–6pm. Bigger post offices are also open on Saturday morning. There are vending machines for stamps outside most post offices. Postage info: *ctt.pt*.

PRICES

The cheapest places to do food shopping on the Algarve are international budget supermarket chains. Museum entrance fees start at 1.50 euros, with reductions for children, students and pensioners. Set menus in simple local restaurants may include a glass of wine and cost as little as 10 euros. Eating out really can pay here!

HOW MUCH DOES IT COST?

Coffee	0.60 euros *for an espresso*
Snack	2.50 euroe *for a* bifana *roll*
Wine	2 euros *for a glass of wine in a bar (red/rosé/ Vinho verde)*
Souvenir	6 euros *for a handpainted azulejo tile*
Public transport	ca. 1.50 euros *for a 10-km train journey*
Bicycle	15 euros *for 1-day mountain- bike hire*

PUBLIC HOLIDAYS

Local holidays honouring the patron saints take place in many towns and villages. The following are national holidays:

1 Jan	Ano Novo (New Year)
Feb/March	Shrove Tuesday
March/April	Good Friday
25 April	Dia de Liberdade
	(Anniversary of the 1974 revolution)
1 May	Dia do Trabalhador (Labour Day)
10 June	Dia de Portugal
	(Portugal Day on the day of death of
	national poet Luís de Camões)
15 Aug	Assumption
5 Oct	Implantação da República
	(founding of the Republic 1910)
1 Nov	All Saints' Day
1 Dec	Restauração da Independência
	(end of the union with Spain 1640)
8 Dec	Imaculada Conceição
	(Immaculate Conception)
25 Dec	Natal (Christmas)

TELEPHONE & INTERNET

The dialling code for Portugal is +351. Mobile numbers begin with a 9 and landlines with a 2. WiFi is available in all hotels and most cafés and restaurants.

TOILETS

Lots of beach bar toilets (and some in older buildings) are unable to process paper. Use the bins provided.

WEATHER

High season
Low season

	JAN	FEB	MARCH	APRIL	MAY	JUNE	JULY	AUG	SEPT	OCT	NOV	DEC
Daytime temperatures (°C)	15°	16°	18°	20°	22°	25°	28°	28°	26°	22°	19°	16°
Night-time temperatures (°C)	9°	10°	11°	13°	14°	18°	20°	20°	19°	16°	13°	10°
☀ Sunshine hours/day	6	7	7	9	10	12	12	12	10	8	6	6
🌦 Rainy days/month	7	6	8	5	3	1	0	0	2	4	7	7
≋ Sea temperatures in °C	15°	15°	15°	16°	17°	18°	19°	20°	20°	19°	17°	16°

☀ Sunshine hours/day   🌦 Rainy days/month   ≋ Sea temperatures in °C

USEFUL WORDS & PHRASES

SMALLTALK

English	Portuguese	Pronunciation
Yes/no/maybe	sim/não/talvez	seeng/nowng/tal'vesh
Please	se faz favor	se fash fa'vor
Thank you	obrigado (m)/obrigada (f)	obri'gadoo/obri'gada
Good morning/Hello/Good afternoon/Goodnight	Bom dia!/Bom dia!/Boa tarde!/Boa noite!	bong 'dia/bong 'dia/'boa 'tard/'boa 'noyt
Hi! Bye!	Olá!/Cião!	o'la/a'dy-oosh
My name is	Chamo-me …	'shamoo-me
What is your name? What is your name (for-mal)?	Como te chamas?/Como se chama?	'komoo te 'shamas/'komoo se 'shama
I am from	Sou de …	so dö e
Sorry! Exucese me	Desculpa!/Desculpe!	dish'kulpa/dish'kulp
Could you repeat?	Como?	'komoo
I don't like this.	(Não) Gosto disto.	(nau) 'goshtoo 'dishtoo
Good/bad	bem/mal	beng/mal

SYMBOLS

EATING & DRINKING

The menu please.	A ementa, se faz favor.	a i'menta, se fash fa'vor
Bottle/glass	garrafa/copo	gar'raffa/'koppoo
Salt/Pepper/sugar	sal/pimenta/açúcar	sall/pi'menta/a'ssookar
Vinegar/oil	vinagre/azeite	vi'nagre/a'zeite
Knife/fork/spoon	faca/garfo/colher	'faka/'garfoo/kool'yer
Milk/cream/lemon	leite/nata/limão	'läite/'nahta/li'mau
With/without ice/gas	com/sem gelo/gás	kong/seng 'zheloo/gash
Vegetarian/allergy	vegetariano, -a/alergia	vezhhetari'anoo, -a/aller'zhia
Bill	conta	konta
The bill, please.	A conta, se faz favor.	a 'konta, se fash fa'vor
Cash/credit card	em dinheiro/com cartão de crédito	end din'yeyroo/kong kar'twong de 'kredit00

MISCELLANEOUS

Where is/ are ...?	Onde é ...?/Onde são ...?	'onde e/'onde sowng
What time is it?	Que horas são?	ke 'orash sowng
It is three o'clock.	São três horas.	sowng tresh 'orash
today/tomorrow/yesterday	hoje/amanhã/ontem	'ozhe/amman'ya/'onteng
How much ...?	Quanto custa ...?	'kwantoo 'kooshta
Where can I access the internet?	Onde há acesso à internet?	'onde a a'ssessoo a 'internet
Help!/Watch out!	Socorro!/Atenção!	soo'korroo/atten'sowng
Fever/pain	febre/dores	'feybre/'doresh
Pharmacy/drugstore	farmácia/drogaria	far'massia/droga'ria
Ban/forbidden	interdição/proibido	interdi'sowng/prooi'bidoo
Broken/working	estragado/não funciona	ishtra'gadoo/nowng fung'siona
Breakdown/garage	avaria/garagem	ava'ria/ga'razheng
Timetable/ticket	horário/bilhete	o'rariyu/bil'yet
0/1/2/3/4/5/6/7/8/9/10/100/1000	zero/um, uma/dois, duas/três/quatro/cinco/seis/sete/oito/nove/dez/cem/mil	'zeroo/'oong, 'ooma/'doysh, 'dooash/tresh/'kwatroo/'seengk'oo/'seysh/'set/'oytoo/'nov/'desh/'seng/meel

HOLIDAY VIBES
FOR RELAXATION & CHILLING

FOR BOOKWORMS & FILMBUFFS

📖 300 DAYS OF SUN

If the title alone isn't enough to sell you a book set in the Algarve, Deborah Lawreson's 2016 tightly plotted novel set in Faro tells the story of two different American visitors to the region across 70 years of history.

📖 PEREIRA MAINTAINS

There are not many English language books set in the Algarve, but to get a fascinating insight into Portugal's history under fascism, you can do a lot worse than Antonio Tabucchi's 1994 masterpiece about a journalist struggling to work in a dictatorship.

🎥 ALGARVE THE MOVIE

Turn up the volume and hit play! A surfer movie about the best surf spots and most remote beaches in the western Algarve. There is no dialogue – the images and background music speak for themselves. (Westcoastcampers, 2014, YouTube)

🎥 ONE FOOT IN THE ALGARVE

One Foot in the Grave may be a tad dated, but Victor Meldrew's disastrous trip to the Algarve will have even the hippest, most up-to-date holiday-makers literally lol-ing over a glass of Algarve wine. (DVD/Streaming, 1993)

PLAYLIST

0:58

‖ SALVADOR SOBRAL – AMAR PELOS DOIS
The soulful winner of Eurovision loves for two in this jazz lament.

▶ NANOOK – MAIS PERTO, SÓ
An Algarve native! With a croaky voice, harmonica and guitar, this Faro songster enchants everyone who gives him a listen.

▶ TIAGO BETTENCOURT – CARTA
A song to give you goose pimples by one of the country's most talented musicians.

▶ ANA MOURA – DESFADO
A bit of fado has to be in this list! Even if this one is probably a touch too cheerful …

▶ ANTONIO VARIAÇÕES – CANÇÃO DO ENGATE
One of many superb songs from this talented singer who died at the tender age of 39.

Your holiday soundtrack can be found on Spotify under MARCO POLO Portugal

Or scan this code with the Spotify app

ONLINE

JOHNNY AFRICA
Johnny Africa's blog entry on the Algarve provides excellent ideas for a trip as well as a whole load of mouth-watering photos! *(johnnyafrica.com/algarve-portugal-itinerary/)*

THE PORTUGALIST
A great guide to the region which also has lots of tips on moving to Portugal should you find yourself wanting more after your holiday *(portugalist.com/the-algarve/)*

ALGARVE BLOG
A blog by two expats with a distinctively artistic slant. Probably no great surprise given that Alyson is a painter and Dave a photographer. Their dog, Kat, plays a pretty major role. *(https://algarve.blog.net)*

O COZINHEIRO ESTE ALGARVE
A blog by a Scottish amateur cook who also runs a guest house near Tavira. Following this blog is one of the easiest ways to try and learn how to cook authentic Algarve food at home *(casa-rosada-algarve.blogspot.com)*

TRAVEL PURSUIT
THE MARCO POLO HOLIDAY QUIZ

Have you worked out what makes the Algarve tick? Use this quiz to test your knowledge about the region's best-kept secrets and most famous facts. The answers are at the bottom of the page, with further information on pages 18–23.

❶ Where does the best wine in the Algarve come from?
a) Lagos
b) Lagoa
c) Loulé

❷ What are most Fado songs about?
a) Sensuousness and eroticism
b) Friends and enemies
c) Longing and love

❸ Which of these flowers is the most valuable?
a) Salt "flowers"
b) Almond flowers
c) Lemon flowers

❹ Why are there so few traces of the Moors left in the Algarve?
a) The Phoenicians needed building material
b) The Romans burned everything
c) The Christians tore everything down and built on top of it

❺ What is Manuelism?
a) A decorative style from the neo-gothic period
b) A carving style from the Renaissance
c) A romantic-era painting style

Which area produces the best wine in the Algarve?

❻ How do birds in the Ria Formosa national park respond to air traffic?
a) Increasingly angrily
b) Very relaxed
c) Moderately over the top

❼ What is on many roofs in the Algarve?
a) A happy seagull family
b) Solar panels
c) A decorative chimney

❽ What does the number on a cork tree mean?
a) It's the year of the last harvest
b) It's the year the tree was planted in the last century
c) It says who owns the tree

❾ Why are fishing boats so colourful?
a) To be seen better in the fog
b) To impress women
c) To scare seagulls

❿ What does the word "azulejo" mean (arabisch *al-zulij*)?
a) Blue tile
b) Small polished stone
c) Gleaming tile

⓫ Why are the villages in the Hinterland getting ever emptier?
a) The inhabitants have drunk too much Medronho
b) There aren't enough donkeys
c) Young people are increasingly drawn to the cities

INDEX

WE WANT TO HEAR FROM YOU!

Did you have a great holiday? Is there something on your mind? Whatever it is, let us know! Whether you want to praise the guide, alert us to errors or give us a personal tip – MARCO POLO would be pleased to hear from you. Please contact us by email

We do everything we can to provide the very latest information for your trip. Nevertheless, despite all of our authors' thorough research, errors can creep in. MARCO POLO does not accept any liability for this.

e-mail: sales@heartwoodpublishing.co.uk

Credits

Cover Picture: Algarve, Beach at sunrise (Getty Images: M. Bottigelli)
Photos: M. Abreu (94/95); DUMONT Bildarchiv: S. Lubenow (Outside front flap, inside front flap,1, 24/25, 50, 78, 92, 121), T.P. Widmann (inside back cover); Getty Images/Blend Images: C. Anderson (35); Getty Images/Moment: S. Cioata (10), Juampiter (72/73), Z. Sanchez (11, 136/137); Getty Images/Photographer's Choice: J. P. Kelly (146/147), huber-images: G. Gräfenhain (102/103), M. Howard (2/3, 14/15, 71, 90/91), S. Lubenow (32/33, 58, 69, 86/87); huber-images/4 Corners: M.Howard (75); Laif: F. Heuer (52, 56), K.-H. Raach (81), C. Zahn (34, 124); S. Lier (151); Look: T. Roetting (88), T. Stankiewicz (105, 129), B. v. Dierendonck (118); Look/age fotostock (141); Look/Cavan Images (8); mauritius images: L. Avers (30/31), F. GUIZIOU (38/39), R. Harding (6/7), Howard (27), M. Howard (12/13, 117), J. Warburton-Lee (126/127); mauritius images/Alamy (19, 20, 23, 48/49, 100, 106, 112), A. Gardiner (132/133), M. Howard (114), S. Reddy (26/27), M. Rodrigues (139), T. E. White (43); mauritius images/Alamy/Amnat99 (44); mauritius images/Alamy/Emmanuel LATTES (108/109); mauritius images/Alamy/GM Photo Images (62); mauritius images/amnat99/Alamy (122); mauritius images/Bildagentur-online/McPhoto-Boyungs/Alamy (47); mauritius images/eye35.pix/Alamy (99); mauritius images/MARKA/ Alamy (31); mauritius images/Travel Collection: G. Lengler (135); mauritius images/Warburton-Lee: S. Lubenow (148/149); Schapowalow: O. Fantuz (64/65); Schapowalow/4 Corners: M. Howard (82/83); Schapowalow/SIME: L. Da Ros (77); T. P. Widmann (9, 61)

4th Edition – fully revised and updated 2022

Worldwide Distribution: Heartwood Publishing Ltd, Bath, United Kingdom
www.heartwoodpublishing.co.uk

© MAIRDUMONT GmbH & Co. KG, Ostfildern
Authors: Sara Lier, Rolf Osang
Editor: Petra Klose
Picture editor: Ina-Marie Inderka
Cartography: © MAIRDUMONT, Ostfildern (pp. 36–37, 128, 131, 134, outer flap, pull-out map) © MAIRDUMONT, Ostfildern, using data from OpenStreetMap, Licence CC-BY-SA 2.0 (pp. 40-41, 42, 54, 66-67, 68, 76, 84, 96-97, 110-111).
Cover design and pull-out map cover design: bilekjaeger_Kreativagentur with Zukunftswerkstatt, Stuttgart
Page design: Langenstein Communication GmbH, Ludwigsburg

Heartwood Publishing credits:
Translated from the German by John Owen, Kathleen Becker, Jennifer Walcoff Neuheiser, Suzanne Kirkbright
Editors: Felicity Laughton, Kate Michell, Sophie Blacksell Jones
Prepress: Summerlane Books, Bath
Printed in India

MARCO POLO AUTHOR
SARA LIER

Sara Lier has been leading tour groups around the Algarve for many years. From the coast to the mountains, from the hinterland to the narrow streets of the towns, she has guided everywhere across the region. Sara loves southern Portugal, where she now lives, both in the quiet winter months and when it is busy in summer!

DOS & DON'TS

HOW TO AVOID SLIP-UPS & BLUNDERS

DON'T SCRAMBLE AROUND ON THE CLIFFS

Erosion has afflicted many cliff sections in the Algarve. The signs on clifftops and on beaches in the Algarve mean what they say. Rocks really do often fall from the cliffs here. If you want to go climbing, find a marked place with supervision.

DON'T PLAY WITH FIRE

You can't be too careful in the dry summer months. Forest fires are a real and present danger here – especially in eucalyptus forests. One cigarette can cause decades of damage.

DON'T SAY "GRACIAS"

You may well be proud of the Spanish you can speak but don't forget Portual was occupied by Spain for a long time so although everyone in Portugal understands Spanish, it can be extremely rude to speak it. "Obrigada" is just as easy to say as "gracias".

DO WALK, DON'T DRIVE IN TOWNS

When building the old towns in Portugal, no one ever imagined cars would exist and the streets show this. Streets get easily blocked and it can be very stressful to drive in them. Find a car park outside and walk if you can.

DO CHECK THE PRICE OF FISH

Fish and seafood are often sold by the kilogram in restaurants. If you get it wrong when ordering, this can mean an embarrassingly big bill. Ask the staff to weigh things before ordering so that you are spared any nasty surprises.